21 Ways

TO BUILD YOUR Business WITH A Book

21 Ways

TO BUILD YOUR

Business

WITH A Book

SECRETS TO DRAMATICALLY GROW YOUR INCOME,
CREDIBILITY, AND CELEBRITY-POWER BY BEING AN AUTHOR

ADAM WITTY

Published by Advantage, Charleston, South Carolina.
Member of Advantage Media Group.

ADVANTAGE is a registered trademark and the Advantage colophon is a trademark of Advantage Media Group, Inc.

Printed in the United States of America.

ISBN: 978-159932-365-7
LCCN: 2012954837

This publication is designed to provide accurate and authoritative information in regard to the subject matter covered. It is sold with the understanding that the publisher is not engaged in rendering legal, accounting, or other professional services. If legal advice or other expert assistance is required, the services of a competent professional person should be sought.

Advantage Media Group is proud to be a part of the Tree Neutral® program. Tree Neutral offsets the number of trees consumed in the production and printing of this book by taking proactive steps such as planting trees in direct proportion to the number of trees used to print books. To learn more about Tree Neutral, please visit **www.treeneutral.com**. To learn more about Advantage's commitment to being a responsible steward of the environment, please visit **www.advantagefamily.com/green**

Advantage Media Group is a publisher of business, self-improvement, and professional development books and online learning. We help entrepreneurs, business leaders, and professionals share their Stories, Passion, and Knowledge to help others Learn & Grow™. Do you have a manuscript or book idea that you would like us to consider for publishing? Please visit **advantagefamily.com** or call **1.866.775.1696.**

I dedicate this book to the people of Advantage Media Group who are dedicated to helping our authors share their Stories, Passion, and Knowledge to help others *Learn & Grow*™.

YOUR OPPORTUNITY TO ACHIEVE MORE

Do you want more from your business? More income? More customers to enjoy working with? New opportunities? Do you want to make an impact?

Your opportunity to accomplish all of this—and more —is here.

Throughout my career, I have had the great fortune to work with people from nearly every type of business, and every walk of life. Entrepreneurs, small business owners, professional speakers, attorneys, doctors, financial advisors, coaches, philanthropists—the list goes on.

The Advantage Media Group team and I have helped them move from entrepreneur to author. I've watched them take their business to the next level, grow their income, and expand their reach by being the authority, celebrity, and expert in their field. I've shared their elation when they hold a copy of their book for the first time.

Most importantly, I have had the great satisfaction of knowing our authors are doing what they've always dreamed of—sharing their *Stories*, *Passion*, and *Knowledge* with the world—and are moving ahead to accomplish even more.

This is the power of a book.

As we move into a new and very different economy today, this magical power of a book is more important than ever. To achieve success, you must be dramatically different and stand apart from the pack. You must be very clear on the value you offer, matching your services and philosophies to the customers you want to attract. You must be recognized as a thought leader. And you must genuinely earn your customers' support.

In the pages ahead, you will see how entrepreneurs, just like you, accomplish these objectives by being the published author of a book. You'll discover how they use books to build their business, and change their lives. Yes, you will have to invest time and money, both while creating your book, and after. But as you will soon read, this investment in your business, your message, and *yourself* is worth every minute— and every penny.

Imagine the possibilities. Then go for it. There is no time like now.

Let's Get Started!

Adam D. Witty

Founder & Chief Executive Officer

Advantage Media Group

awitty@advantageww.com

843.701.4943

TABLE OF CONTENTS

CHAPTER 1   15

Create Loyal Clients and Watch Your Profits Grow

How a Book Fosters Dedication and Passion—and Turns Clients into Fans

CHAPTER 2   23

Be the Company Your Prospects Go to First

Increase Your Visibility, Credibility, and Clout with a Book

CHAPTER 3   31

An Easy Way to Get New Customers Who Are Five Times More Valuable to Your Business

Increase the Quantity and Quality of Referrals to Your Company with a Book

CHAPTER 4   39

Could You Use an Extra $1,000 Every Month?

How to Create Passive Income Streams with a Book

CHAPTER 5   49

Get the Media Coverage and Free Publicity You've Dreamed of

How to Use Your Book to Become a Darling of the Media

CHAPTER 6   57

Can One Lead Result in Over $150,000 in New Business?

How a Book Makes it Easier to Attract New Customers and Increase Revenues

CHAPTER 7   65

How to Leverage Your Marketing Dollars

Use a Book to Reach More Prospects and Get a Better Rate of Return

CHAPTER 8   73

How to Harness Celebrity Power to Build Your Business

From National TV to Local Radio—Be a Celebrity with Your Book

CHAPTER 9   79

Find Prospects Who Are Ready to Buy Without Salespeople

How to Use Your Book to Pre-sell Prospects and Gain New Customers

CHAPTER 10   87

Are You Reaching Your Target Audience?

How to Cut Through the Noise and Influence Your Prospects

CHAPTER 11   95

Your Vehicle to Create an Impact While Increasing Your Income

Parlay Your Message into Business Success

CHAPTER 12   101

The Secret to Creating a Strong, Revenue Generating Company

Achieve Business Victory by Motivating Employees and Customers

CHAPTER 13   107

Be on Par with Industry Giants

How to Level the Playing Field and Rise Above the Competition

CHAPTER 14   117

Have Plenty of Money to Do What You Want to Do

Achieve Success in Business, Philanthropy, or Both, with a Book

CHAPTER 15   125

What Legacy Will You Leave?

How to Make a Lasting Impact Through Your Book

CHAPTER 16   131

An Easier Way to Create New Connections and Revenue Streams

Use Your Book to Find Business Partners, Joint Ventures, and New Opportunities

CHAPTER 17   139

Everything You Need on a Business Card and More

Give Prospects Your Contact Information and Unique Selling Proposition with Your Book

CHAPTER 18   147

Motivated Customers Who Buy and Reduced Competition

How to Create a Brand that People Recognize and Value

CHAPTER 19   155

Create Your Own Money Printing Machine

Use a Book to Acquire Leads and Build Your List

CHAPTER 20   163

Secrets of Highly Paid Speakers

How to Be In Demand, Command Higher Fees, and Enjoy Motivated Audiences

CHAPTER 21   173

The Secret to Creating Multiple Revenue Streams in Your Business

How to Generate New Business with a Book

CHAPTER 22   181

How to Write a Book—Quickly and Easily—On a Businessperson's Schedule

You Can Be a Published Author Even if You're Not a "Born Writer"

ABOUT THE AUTHOR   195

Adam Witty

RESOURCES   197

Register Your Book

REGISTER YOUR BOOK

AND ACCESS FREE RESOURCES FOR POTENTIAL AUTHORS!

It doesn't matter where you are in the world, Adam can help you share your Stories, Passion, and Knowledge with the world in the form of a published book.

Visit **THE21WAYSBOOK.COM/REGISTER** to
access these free resources:

 RECEIVE a subscription to the Author Success University™ and Insights with Experts™ monthly teleseminars wherein successful authors and book marketing experts reveal their tips and tricks for marketing and growing a business with a book

 REGISTER for a webinar led by Adam Witty: "How to Quickly Write, Publish, And Profit From A Book That Will Explode Your Business"

 COMPLETE Advantage's Publishing Questionnaire and receive a complimentary Discovery Call with an acquisitions editor to help you determine if your ideas, concepts, or manuscript are worth turning into a book

ACCESS ALL OF THE ABOVE FREE RESOURCES BY REGISTERING YOUR BOOK AT

THE21WAYSBOOK.COM/REGISTER

21 Ways

Create Loyal Clients and Watch Your Profits Grow

How a Book Fosters Dedication and Passion—and Turns Clients into Fans

Create Loyal Clients and Watch Your Profits Grow

How a Book Fosters Dedication and Passion—and Turns Clients into Fans

When Dr. Leslie Van Romer wrote her book, she never thought it would put her in the league of the world's most powerful companies. After all, when you think of the most successful businesses today, what comes to mind? Apple? Amazon? Or, if you're a die-hard online shopper, perhaps Zappos?

However, by writing a book, the chiropractor, nutrition expert, and Advantage author used the same client-building techniques as these multi-national corporations. And by using these techniques, Leslie grew her business. To see the connection, let's step back and take a closer look at the corporations I just mentioned.

First, consider what these companies have in common. Of course, great products would be one factor. Superb service, another. In fact Zappos states, loud and clear, "Powered by Service," right in their logo. You can probably name more commonalities, but all would point to one, overriding characteristic. Each company has a fanatical customer base who will shop *nowhere* else. They are true fans who not only buy products, they shout from the mountaintops, exalting the company to anyone who will listen.

The most profitable companies in the world boast the most fanatical clients and customers. In fact, there is a direct correlation between fanatical clients and profit. Apple, for example, reported a record-setting net profit of $13.06 billion in the first quarter of 2012. Amazon came in at $13.2 billion, above analysts' expectations.

Now, a fanatical customer base exists for two main reasons:

1. Everything that anyone does in successful companies revolves around a mission to serve the customer *first*.

2. These companies are very clear about *communicating* this mission to their audience.

Zappos, for example, goes well beyond stating customer service standards on their website. The company has several blogs with topics ranging from fashion culture to messages from the "Zappos family." Their expo site is "dedicated to showcasing the innovative work happening at Zappos." The reason for communicating this way is simple. By providing more content, they deliver more value to the customer. They are creating a "family" and customers want to be a part of it. Customers feel connected.

There is another benefit beyond creating a connection with your customers. For service providers, such as doctors, lawyers, or information marketers, additional information makes it more likely your clients will succeed with the material you teach or provide. Clear and detailed information results in understanding. You develop a relationship of trust, especially when you let your personality show. Your clients are far more likely to comply with your instructions. They go beyond the point of being good customers, to becoming true fans.

At this point, you may be making the connection from global corporation to local chiropractor. Leslie shares her message and philosophy about weight loss with her patients in her book, and they *love* it. Even the title is fun, *Getting Into Your Pants*. Leslie explains it this way:

"What they love the most about Getting Into Your Pants, *besides being fun, simple, and practical, is that it's written in conversational language and sounds just like me talking directly to them. Now, they can take me home and be with me any time they want, so they tell me. They are so tickled that their chiropractor is also an author and a motivational health speaker. The book has added depth and breadth to my relationships with my patients and, as we all know, connected relationships are at the core of every successful business."*

BRIAN FRICKE
Orlando, Florida

Stronger client relationships are important to Brian Fricke, as well. Brian is a financial planner and author of Advantage published, *Worry Free Retirement—Do What You Want, When You Want, Where You Want.* Shortly after releasing his book, Brian provided a copy to every client. He had an important reason for doing this. "Clients can get a flavor of who I am and our philosophies. Therefore, it tends to create a stronger bond between us."

Fitness guru, Jennifer Nicole Lee, is a three-time Advantage author who agrees with this sentiment. She recently told me why: "I think my customers, especially the women, become more empowered. You're really able to win over their minds and hearts. When you can win over your customer's heart, and really connect with them, let them know you're there to help them, they'll continue to come back to you."

Advantage author and chiropractor, Dr. Sonia Kwapisinksi, had an "ah-ha" moment when working with her patients.

"After being asked the same questions from my patients, time after time, I realized that I needed to put something in print. Not only to avoid repetition, but to show my patients that the information I was giving them was fact, and that it worked."

For all of these authors, sharing their message with clients has benefited them in even greater ways. I think Jennifer sums it up well. "Your customers continue to talk about you. They'll tell their best friend, their mom, their daughter to 'read this book, and go get her products.' It's a trickle down or domino effect. The book starts that natural organic marketing that your customers do for you."

A book is one of the best tools to reinforce your viewpoints and message. And by sharing your beliefs, you create the glue that bonds you with your clients and customers. However, there is yet another way you can use a book to benefit both your customers and your business.

THE UNEXPECTED BENEFIT OF A GIFT—
FOR YOU AND YOUR CUSTOMERS

Let's go back to our multinational corporations again. These companies use another technique that helps to grow a passionate fan base. This technique is a *systematic plan* to show appreciation to clients.

Now think for a moment about all of the companies that have sent you gifts in appreciation for your business. That thought is over pretty quickly, is it not? Few businesses do this. And since few businesses do, this is an even greater reason why *you should*. It is an easy way to stand out among your competitors.

Naturally, this begs the question…what do I give? Why not a copy of your book? Books are fabulous client gifts for an important reason. As a society, we place a high value on books. It may be $15, $20, even $30, depending on the book, but we attach a price to it. When someone gives us a book, we read it, add it to our library, or share it with a friend. It goes well beyond the free information you can find just about anywhere today.

A book is an important tool in any sound customer-appreciation system. Giving your book to clients communicates thoughtfulness on your part. It also provides a platform for your message, beliefs, and for *you*. It strengthens your connection with clients and customers, making you a valued part of their life.

Coach, speaker, and Advantage author, Chris Ruisi, experienced this benefit by sharing his book, *Step Up and Play Big*, with clients. Since then, several have given his book glowing reviews on Amazon. Chris is not only furthering his relationship with clients, he is promoting his book at the same time.

At Advantage, we can help you find your unique message and create *your* fan base with a book. You may not have as many fans as Apple, but they *will* help you grow your business. Take the first step by completing our publishing questionnaire at advantagefamily.com or calling 866.775.1696.

21
Ways

Be the Company Your Prospects Go to First

Increase Your Visibility, Credibility, and Clout with a Book

Be the Company Your Prospects Go to First

Increase Your Visibility, Credibility, and Clout with a Book

Have you ever wondered how you can possibly stand out among the crowd and noise of your competition?

With over seven billion world residents and 300 million folks in the United States, it's easy to feel like a grain of sand on a beach. And it seems like *everyone* these days has websites, blogs, free reports, videos, webinars, free CDs, and more.

Now don't get me wrong, these are important and useful marketing tools, and you *should* use them. But you need something *more* to elevate your business above the crowd and make you the logical choice—the "go-to" company in your niche or industry.

That something is a book authored by *you*.

Think of it this way, while there are over seven billion world residents, there are only about three million authors.

This means that, as a published author, you are part of the top 0.04% of the global population. How is *that* for differentiation?

Being an author instantly makes you an expert. It catapults you ahead of "the pack." As an author, you are no longer a "me too."

KEITH AYERS
Harrisburg, Pennsylvania

Take Keith Ayers, for example. Keith is a business consultant, coach, and Advantage author of *Engagement is Not Enough – You Need Passionate Employees to Reach Your Dream.* When he brought his new book home, he had an interesting, yet not surprising, reaction from his daughter:

> "When my book first arrived, I took a few copies home and showed one to my then 17-year-old daughter. She said, 'This is weird.' I said, 'Why is it weird?' She said, 'It's just weird that my dad has got a book out.' Her father, in her mind,

did not fit into the context of an author. Anytime I meet someone new and they find out that I have a published book, it changes the conversation. From a personal point of view, and a business point of view, having a book has been extremely positive."

Keith is experiencing the phenomenon I call the "author aura." Prospects, clients, and customers see you as more credible than your competitors. You suddenly have elevated status. Why? Well, I like the explanation given by another Advantage author, Pat Williams. Now, any sports fan will likely recognize his name since Pat is the co-founder of the Orlando Magic basketball team. He has more than 70 books published by now, and is planning to write more. Pat explains it this way:

"Once published, in the eyes of many you're an expert, and you should be. You've got to be passionate to write and publish a book."

At this point, you may be thinking to yourself, "Well I don't need to be *the* expert in my industry (or town, or niche). Our service speaks for itself. Our staff has certified training. We use only the best parts. We have the highest standards." And I'm sure you can think of additional similar statements, depending on your industry.

Unfortunately, every time you say this, you can bet, *your competition is saying it, too.*

SO WHAT ARE YOU DOING THAT IS DIFFERENT OR SPECIAL? HOW CAN YOU ENSURE THAT PROSPECTS WILL CHOOSE YOU OVER YOUR COMPETITION?

This question is especially important if you sell commodities, or if you own a commoditized business. This includes doctors, attorneys, dentists, financial advisors, appliance or HVAC repair companies, collision specialists, and so on. It is even more critical for you to differentiate yourself in these over-crowded markets.

A book does the heavy lifting when it comes to differentiation. In addition to giving you the "author aura," a book allows you to speak directly to prospects in your niche. After reading your book, your prospects identify with you. They hear your message and feel they actually *know* you. It's not surprising that you become the logical choice, even when there are several other businesses to choose from.

Dr. Scot Gray is a perfect example of this. Scot recently published a book with Advantage called *Good Back, Bad Back – The 10 Things Women Must Know to Eliminate Back Pain and Look and Feel Younger*. When you read this title, it's easy to see who Scot is targeting for business. With this book, he is speaking directly to potential customers. By providing information and showing his personality, women will be more comfortable choosing Scot as their chiropractor.

Scot's book has helped him to stand out in another way. Out of curiosity, I recently searched Yellowpages.com for chiropractors in the Columbus, Ohio area. I wasn't surprised when my search resulted in 263 names! So, I decided to do a bit more research. Well, actually, I had my assistant spend the afternoon checking the website of every practice on that list. Out of the 263 chiropractors, Scot is the *only* author. This is very important because, for many consumers, being an author is the tipping point for choosing *you* over any other business. As Scot says, "People assume you know what you're talking about because you're an author of a book." This is critical when consumers are trying to choose between businesses that all seem to be the same.

Construction Risk Advisor and Advantage author, Robert Phelan, knows this well. His book, *Broke: The Broken Contractors Insurance System and How to Fix It*, is the marketing tool that sets him apart from competition in the insurance industry. As he says, "Insurance is a commodity and a boring commodity at that. My book is a conversation starter, a point of differentiation, and a credibility and expertise builder that has gotten me into the C-Suites of prospective clients."

Lawyer and professional speaker, John Patrick Dolan, is another Advantage author who uses books to enhance his expert status and reduce the "commoditization" of his business. John is a criminal law specialist who maintains a busy legal practice, a professional speaking business, *and* a continuing legal education center. He has authored several books beginning with his premier work, *Negotiate Like the Pros*. John views his books as critical positioning tools for everything he does. "My books have positioned me to be highly paid as a professional speaker, to be highly paid as a legal practitioner, and to attract people who attend our continuing education center seminars. My books prove I have expertise and people recognize that."

No matter what business you're in, one thing is clear: consumers no longer settle for average service or the best price. They simply have too many choices. Being an author makes you *different*. You exceed expectations of both prospects and customers because you have gone the extra mile. I think recent Advantage author Henry Evans sums it up best, "There's nothing better than a book for the credibility, the authority, and the ability to be an established expert."

At Advantage, we can help you publish a book that will position you as the first choice in your industry. Contact us at advantagefamily.com to begin. Yes, writing a book takes some effort, but it will pay off for you—time and time again.

21

Ways

An Easy Way to Get New Customers Who Are Five Times More Valuable to Your Business

Increase the Quantity and Quality of Referrals to Your Company with a Book

An Easy Way to Get New Customers Who Are Five Times More Valuable to Your Business

Increase the Quantity and Quality of Referrals to Your Company with a Book

Did you know there is an easy, yet often overlooked, method for acquiring new customers? And what if I told you these customers will, on average, spend *five times more* with your business than a customer you acquire through general marketing or advertising?

This gold mine of new customers comes from *referrals*. Surprised? Many business owners are. Yet, the most profitable businesses report that well over 70% of new clients result from referrals made by current customers.

So why are referred customers so valuable? When prospects arrive to your business from referrals, they are essentially pre-sold. A referral from a friend or family member validates that you and your business are the real deal. Your new prospect believes you'll do everything you say you will, and then some. They arrive at your business with a sense of trust, even respect. They are much easier to convince, they are ready to buy, and they are willing to spend more money.

As a rule of thumb, studies show that roughly 20% of your clients will freely give referrals without your asking. Another 20% will not give referrals at all. But that leaves 60% of your clients who will likely refer you and your business *if you ask them.*

With advertising rising in cost and often producing lackluster results, referrals are one of your best and most cost effective marketing tools. Put another way, your customers and clients are doing your marketing for you. If you can choose only *one* marketing task in your week, it should be to make it easier for clients to refer business to you.

Nearly every Advantage author has increased referrals to their business with their book and grown their income as a result. And they've done it both online and offline. Now, online referrals often occur from person to person, but the rubber *really* hits the road when a guru with a strong, loyal following endorses your book. Think about it. If you agree with someone's philosophies, you are more apt to follow their recommendations. Their endorsement is often just as strong as one provided by a friend. In addition, their referral reaches thousands of people at one time. Talk about benefiting your business!

Pat Williams uses this strategy to promote his books with great success. "Get books into the hands of chatterboxes. If you can get the army of cheerleaders talking about your book, or Tweeting, or emailing, that's the ultimate."

Offline referrals are just as effective and, in my opinion, even easier to get. An easy way to start is to give copies of your book to clients, and then ask them to pass a copy along to friends, family, and colleagues. The book instantly

Adam Witty with Advantage author and Co-Founder of the Orlando Magic, Pat Williams

creates a "conversation starter" for your clients when they talk with friends. In essence, you have greased the skids, making it easier for your clients to give referrals.

Financial planner Brian Fricke is a master at this strategy. Brian gives every client two copies of his book with the request to pass it on to any friends or family members who might need his help. Thanks to this strategy, several referrals have become new clients.

Brian also enjoys another benefit from client referrals. He tells us that, thanks to his book, referred prospects are more qualified and ready to work with him. "One chapter in the book is titled 'If I Ran the Country for a Day.' In it, I rant and rave and give people a sense of me. I know it attracts people because they have commented on it. But I'm sure it turns people off, too. But that's OK. It saves time for everybody."

In addition to giving your book to clients, you can also use it directly in your retail business. Carl Sewell used this technique to help grow his business from three auto dealers to *18*. It began in 1990, when Carl wrote *Customers for Life: How to Turn That One Time Buyer into a Lifetime Customer.* In the book, he details his company's "Ten Commandments of Customer Service." Carl then began leaving several copies of his book in the waiting rooms at his dealership. More importantly, he instructed each salesperson to give a free copy to anyone who came in for a test drive. On script, they would say, "Thank you so much for coming in to test drive one of our cars. As a small token of our appreciation, our founder and CEO would like you to have an autographed copy of his book, *Customers for Life.*"

Now, after people got home, most would at least flip through the book if they didn't read it. Yet even by flipping through pages, they could see Carl's strong customer service philosophy. Naturally, most would think, "Wow, this is a dealership that really knows how to take care of customers!" As a result, more people returned to buy a car from Carl's dealership, citing the book as an important factor in their decision.

However, another interesting thing happened. Sometimes potential customers did *not* buy, often because they decided to purchase another brand of vehicle. However, they would still pass the book onto friends, neighbors, and family members who were interested in the cars sold at Carl's dealership. There were several occasions when potential customers came into the dealership with a copy of *Customers for Life* in their hands. They would tell the sales reps that a neighbor had referred them, even though that neighbor had *never* purchased a car from Carl. The book's message was so strong, it compelled people who had only passed through the dealership to make referrals.

This leads me to the second slam-dunk when it comes to using your book for referrals. With a book, you have more control over the message your clients share. Although your clients may love doing business with you, this does not guarantee they'll deliver your "30-second commercial" in good form. In fact, your best clients may be driving prospects away by saying the wrong things unintentionally. However, with a book, you can often make up for these mistakes. Your book is your scripted masterpiece; the same masterpiece your referrals will read. It virtually guarantees that potential clients will get the exact message you want them to hear.

Many business owners try to boost referrals by offering discounts, or other incentives. While this may encourage customers to *give* the referral, it does not guarantee your message will be correct. The value of receiving a book, along with the helpful information inside, overcomes this obstacle. It makes it easy for your customers to strike up a conversation when they refer friends to your business.

Ignoring referrals for your business will cost you plenty. With a book, you can encourage not only the quantity of referrals but the quality as well. Contact us by visiting advantagefamily.com. We'll be happy to show you how referrals are just one of the many ways to grow your business—and your income—with a book.

21 Ways

Could You Use an Extra $1,000 Every Month?

How to Create Passive Income Streams with a Book

Could You Use an Extra $1,000 Every Month?

How to Create Passive Income Streams with a Book

Imagine having an extra $1,000 flowing into your business every month, yet doing little work to earn it. Extra money that you could use to hire an assistant, pay the insurance bill, or give yourself a long-overdue raise. Any successful business owner would agree; passive income is something to strive for. And a book is a definite way to achieve it. Dozens of Advantage authors earn far more than an extra $1,000 every month, and you can too.

You can generate passive income for yourself, your charity, or your business in ways you would expect such as selling your book in both retail and online bookstores. However, you can also make money with methods you may not have thought of such as back-of-the-room sales or corporate and specialty deals.

So, let's start with the obvious. Thousands of authors sell their books through bookstores such as Barnes & Noble or Books-A-Million. Mass retailers such as Wal-Mart, Target, and others offer even more opportunities. In addition, there is the world of online commerce, which is becoming a larger component of overall book sales every year.

Your opportunities to make money certainly don't end with traditional online and offline booksellers. Nowadays, you can sell your books in airports, train stations, hospitals, museums, and much more. Every day, it seems as though another retailer begins to sell books. There are extensive opportunities here, especially if your book speaks to a specific niche that uses, or benefits from, one of these less traditional retailers.

Pat Williams advocates this "less traditional" approach. He cites author Rich Wolfe's strategy as an example. When beloved Philadelphia Phillies broadcaster Harry Kalas died suddenly at the beginning of the 2009 season, it was front-page news throughout Pennsylvania. Rich compiled stories about Harry from colleagues, players, coaches, and friends. His book, *Remembering Harry Kalas – Wonderful Stories from Friends About a Great Life*, was released a year later. In addition to selling his book through traditional routes, he made a deal to sell it in a chain of convenience outlets on the East Coast. Thanks to this strategy, Rich sold 50,000 books in Philadelphia alone.

However, sales in stores, traditional or otherwise, are not the only way to create new income streams. Many authors become speakers after publishing a book. I believe that every speaker should author and every author should speak. Speaking is not only a fantastic way to promote your book; it's a great way to generate income, both through speaking fees and back-of-the-room sales.

Here's how it works. After you speak, your audience will want more. And the best way to take a piece of you home is to purchase your book at the back of the room. **There are dozens of Advantage authors that easily earn six figures annually just by selling books this way.**

Advantage author, Steve Gilliland, uses his books with a dramatic effect on his company's income. Steve, author of *Enjoy the Ride*, *Mum's the Word*, *Making a Difference*, *Performance Essentials in the Workplace*, and *License to Chill*, reports that his company generates a high six-figure income annually *from book sales alone.* He uses several innovative strategies to accomplish this:

Advantage author, Steve Gilliland, speaks at The Society for Human Resource Management.

"We sell a lot of books in the back of the room after I have finished speaking. From the manner in which we display them to the marketing materials we use to promote them,

people are drawn to the table to leaf through the books. Additionally, every person who hears me speak is given a high quality bookmark with ordering information on the reverse side. We have several 'order triggers' on the product tables, which allow people to either download the books or order them at their convenience online. We also have a defined pre-purchase program that makes copies of my books available to every person who attends my presentation."

Almon Gunter is another Advantage author who uses a similar strategy. Almon is a former Olympic qualifying athlete turned motivational speaker. When hired for a speaking engagement, Almon arranges to sell books in the back of the room. He combines book sales with motivational materials such as audio programs, workbooks, and posters. Almon only needs to sell 40 to 50 books to put an extra $1,000 in his pocket. This is in addition to his speaking fee, and as he says, "It just provides extra income."

While extra income is an exciting result for any speaker, there is an extra bonus from back-of-the-room sales. Sales coach and speaker, Steve Clark, finds that his books add to the buyer experience. Steve is the author of Advantage published *Profitable Persuasion*. He recently told me why he feels this type of sale is so important.

"I display and sell books at the back of the room anytime I am speaking. I also autograph them. It produces a little extra income, but as much as anything else, it is part of

the experience that people get when they hear me speak. It enhances their experience and also adds to anything I said at the front of the room."

So, in addition to generating extra income from book sales, Steve develops relationships with his customers turning some from book buyers into future clients.

Professional photographer, David Johnson, has benefitted from back-of-the-room sales, both professionally and personally. David is passionately devoted to raising funds for the people of Sudan. Thanks to his Advantage published books, *Voices of Sudan* and *Voices of Beauty*, David has increased his number of speaking engagements, raised his fees, sold more books, and sold "thousands of dollars worth of prints." All of this generates more funds for his foundation, Silent Images. He has raised money to provide Darfur residents with wells, medicines, and food. Yet it doesn't end there. The exposure David has received due to his book and speaking engagements has benefitted his photography business as well. This extra income allows David to devote more time doing what he loves, advocating for the people of Sudan.

However, selling books and other items after speaking is not the only way to create more income for your business or passion. Have you ever thought that a certain company would really benefit if they purchased your book? This is not such a crazy idea. We classify this category as sales to non-bookstore and non-retail markets. Thousands of companies buy bulk quantities of books every year for use as premiums, gifts, employee training, marketing tools, and more. There are so many topics and types of books that appeal to corporations and businesses; it's impossible to list them here. But whatever the topic, corporate sales result in hundreds, and even thousands, of books being sold at one time. As you can imagine, this can be very lucrative for you as an author and your business.

"Rights" sales are another opportunity altogether. This includes selling foreign translation rights of your book in other countries, documentary or film rights, and the lesser-known option of licensing rights. Although this may seem like an unreachable goal at first thought, you may be surprised. Authors of training books, for example, will sell companies, coaches, or other trainers the right to use and sell the book as their own. And this is just one of many options.

Finally, I want to mention one additional benefit. Your book can provide a platform for unexpected avenues to grow your business. Although this isn't really passive income, it is a way to expand your business, and create new revenues at the same time. Nearly every Advantage author has done this in one way or another:

- Jelynne Jardiniano, author of *Restaurant from Scratch – How to Trust Your Heart, Listen to the Market, and Beat the Odds*, has grown her restaurant business and is now developing a documentary about restaurant start-ups.

- Ghislaine Labelle expanded her speaking career after writing her book, *Calming the Waters at Work – How to Deal with Workplace Conflicts.*
- And Linda Hancock's book, *Life is an Adventure,* has enabled her to expand her private psychology practice and develop training teleseminars for other professionals.

These are just a few of the countless examples of Advantage authors using their books as springboards to create new business opportunities and income. Let us help you do the same. Visit advantagefamily.com to start the process now.

21
Ways

Get the Media Coverage and Free Publicity You've Dreamed Of

How to Use Your Book to Become a Darling of the Media

Get the Media Coverage and Free Publicity You've Dreamed Of

How to Use Your Book to Become a Darling of the Media

Tara Kennedy-Kline wrote her Advantage published book, *Stop Raising Einstein*, to further a cause that is close to her heart. She never dreamed it would land her a seven-minute segment on *The Today Show*. Yet this is exactly what happened, and it elevated her business, and her cause, as a result.

It all began when her youngest son, Alex, was diagnosed with Asperger's Syndrome. After struggling to cope with his behavior, she discovered that Alex responded to the language and questions she used with her coaching clients. They began journaling together with Tara recording Alex's thoughts and answers. This process helped Alex so much, she decided to write a book to help other families dealing with Asperger's. Thus, *Stop Raising Einstein* came to be.

After publishing her book, Advantage author Tara Kennedy-Kline appeared on The Today Show

Tara also became involved with the National Autism Association and they featured her book in a related trade journal. This is where it gets interesting. *The Today Show* had decided to do a segment on Asperger's Syndrome. One of the show's producers was conducting research for the segment, when he came across the article featuring Tara and her book. This led to an invitation to Tara and her family to appear on *The Today Show*. They had a seven-minute spot, where they talked about their life and coping with Asperger's.

Following this appearance, Tara expanded her business to include coaching, speaking, selling educational toys, and more. She is also a spokesperson for children with Asperger's and their families. And all of this began with her book.

Many entrepreneurs and business owners dream about being interviewed by Oprah, getting a profile in *Inc.* magazine, or landing the guest host spot on CNBC's *Power Lunch*. At the very least, they hope for a feature in their industry trade journals and publications. They know the press is looking for story ideas and sources. In fact, radio alone interviews over 10,000 people every single day. Yet for most entrepreneurs, their dream of publicity remains just a dream. Why?

The answer is simple. Sending press releases and hoping for coverage just doesn't cut it anymore. The media is inundated with press releases every day. Yet most of what they see is the same old thing. Most folks don't realize the media is *not* interested in them. They only care about delivering good content to their readers, viewers, or listeners. If you want to stand out, you have to give the media something new to talk about or a great story. A book does this and more.

When you're an author, you are considered an expert. As David Johnson, Advantage author of *Voices of Sudan,* says, "a book gives you instant credibility." Reporters love interviewing credible experts for their stories whether for radio, TV, print, or online. It makes their job easier because they can develop a story faster. David, by the way, has had interviews with National Public Radio, Radio Disney, Fox News; had articles in several local newspapers; and landed speaking engagements at New York University, UC Berkeley, Georgetown, Stanford, and more. This wouldn't have happened without his book.

This process works with any type of media. Linda Franklin, Advantage author of *Don't Ever Call Me Ma'am – The Real Cougar Woman's Handbook,* knows this firsthand.

Thanks to her book, she is now an established spokesperson for the *New York Times* on topics that appeal to women over 40. So how did she do it?

First, Linda tapped into a conversation that is already going on in the minds of many women. Like Linda, most women over 40 are passionate about living a full life. She validated these feelings in her book, which created interest as well as a following.

After publishing her book, Linda mailed copies to editors at several newspapers including the *New York Times*. When they decided to run an article on the older woman-younger man relationship dynamic, Linda was the obvious choice as an expert. Several of Linda's quotes appeared in this article, and the *New York Times* continues to use Linda as a spokesperson for various topics relating to women over 40.

Brian Fricke's book generated publicity, but through a different route. His book title, *Worry Free Retirement*, was an easy find for reporters using "retirement" in their online search. The subtitle, *Do What You Want, When You Want, Where You Want*, made Brian and his book even more intriguing. As a result, he snared interviews with the Fox Business website as well as *Smart Money* magazine.

A book generates publicity for anyone, in any profession even for people who appear *not* to need it. Advantage author, Steve Sax, is a great example of this. After retiring from 18 years in baseball, Steve was a contributing analyst for Fox Sports' *Prime Time*. He has also appeared as a guest star on several television shows. You would think it would be easy for him to get publicity for anything he does.

However, when Steve wanted to promote his speaking and coaching business, he decided to write a book. It was a wise decision. Although he published *Shift – Change Your Mindset and Change Your World* in 2009, Steve continues to enjoy regular radio and TV interviews about his book to this day. He recently told me, "My book has been a great lead generator and a source of free publicity. And it's been good for sales, too."

JIM ZIEGLER
Atlanta, Georgia

Now if you think books will help you only with national or well-known media, I'd like to tell you about another Advantage author Jim Ziegler, author of *The Prospertiy Equation*. Jim is a consultant for automobile dealers. Years ago, after writing his book, he mailed a copy to the editor of *Dealer Magazine*, the largest magazine for automotive dealers in the country. The editor liked his book, so he invited Jim to write an editorial for the following issue. The editorial was so well received, the editor asked Jim to write a regular monthly column.

From 1997 to 2011, if you flipped through the pages of *Dealer Magazine*, you'd see Jim's two-page column, "Dealer Advocate," in every issue. And at the bottom of each column you'd find Jim's contact information, targeted to automotive dealers, the very people who hire him.

By the way, Jim was an absolute unknown to *Dealer Magazine* until he mailed them a review copy of his book. The book ignited the spark that lead to his monthly column. His consulting business has since skyrocketed. He has also developed several information products and moved into speaking. In fact, he was recently the keynote speaker at the National Automotive Dealer Association conference.

No matter what your goal, a book has phenomenal power to get you in front of the media. Think of the business you'll get when you're a columnist in your industry's largest trade journal. Imagine the exposure to potential donors when a superstar blogger features your cause. From local newspapers to national TV, a book opens media doors.

Whether you're a published author, or just starting to write, it's never too late—or early—to plan for media coverage through your book. We can help you get the media exposure you dream of, as we have with hundreds of authors, whether you've published with us, or not. Take the first step by visiting advantagefamily.com.

CHAPTER 6

21
Ways

Can One Lead Result in Over $150,000 in New Business?

How a Book Makes it Easier to Attract New Customers and Increase Revenues

Can One Lead Result in Over $150,000 in New Business?

How a Book Makes it Easier to Attract New Customers and Increase Revenues

Generating leads or attracting new customers is something any business owner must do—myself included. Unfortunately, many business owners are doing the same things as everyone else. The result is often a disappointing trickle of new leads that you have to work *hard* to sell your services to. Wouldn't it be nice to attract new prospects that are interested and *ready* to do business with you? And to have that incoming flow of prospects be more like a torrent than a trickle?

Advantage authors use their books to generate not only a volume of new leads but *qualified* leads as well. Potential customers seek them out after reading their books or after finding their messages through publicity made possible by their books. These qualified leads are not only ready to buy; they're ready to buy *more*. It's this type of lead that made the headline for this chapter possible for author, Keith Ayers.

As I mentioned in an earlier chapter, Keith is a consultant who works with businesses to develop high-performing teams. Thanks to his book, he has appeared in several journals and newspapers. *USA Today* was one of the publications that quoted him in an article. And from that *one* quote, he received a call from a multi-national company. As Keith says, "I've been working with that company for about 18 months, which has been *worth over $150,000 so far*, and that is going to be ongoing. And that's just one lead."

STEVE CLARK
Pensacola, Florida

Author Steve Clark experienced a similar situation thanks to another unforeseen chain of events. After publishing his book, Steve sent a copy to the editor of his local newspaper.

The paper ran a story in the business section, which caught the attention of the Chamber of Commerce. The Chamber then asked Steve to speak at their business luncheon. One of the attendees was so impressed; he hired Steve to help his company. The result was a $45,000 contract from that one speaking engagement, thanks to his book.

Imagine. One qualified lead, with $45,000, even $150,000, flowing into your business. This is *not* a fluke.

Financial planner, Brian Fricke, will generate far more income than that due to his book. I mentioned earlier how Brian uses his book to generate referrals from existing customers. At last count, Brian had obtained five new clients directly from the book. Now that may not sound like many, but one client is worth $10,000 annually to Brian. Multiply that by five, and you have $50,000 *per year* in new revenues. Multiply that by the number of years Brian will likely serve these clients and you can see how high this figure will climb.

From new clients to sizable contracts, books create endless growth opportunities for your business and your income. Advantage author and marriage counselor, Burrow Hill, views his book, *Talk Tools*, as "the cornerstone" of his business for this reason. Burrow told me that thanks to his book:

> *"Results continue to mount up. I have now been signed with a speaking company who would not have been interested in me without the book. I have co-hosted a couples retreat at a national resort, been interviewed on national radio shows*

four times, been interviewed on Internet TV, have launched a host of related products and the book is being considered for the pre-marital program of a large church."

And what about other authors? How have their businesses grown due to new leads and customers? Well, consider these examples:

- Texas auto dealer, Carl Sewell, grew his business to 18 dealerships spread throughout Dallas, Fort Worth, San Antonio, Grapevine, and Plano.
- Psychologist, Linda Hancock, has expanded her practice, advanced her speaking business, and developed a teleseminar series to train other professionals.
- Speaker and Advantage author, Robert Lemon, has received calls from government agencies and libraries. Both are buying copies of his book, *Now is Your Time*, to give to employees or include in their collections.

The number of ways you can use a book to acquire clients is limited only by your imagination. You can hold a client appreciation party, and provide complimentary copies of your book as parting gifts.

Another idea is to personally deliver or mail a copy of your book to your best potential prospects. Better yet, send your book to the most influential companies and people in your industry. Give your book to current customers, along with an incentive to refer new clients to your business. If you have a retail business, give a copy to every serious customer that walks through your door.

These are just a few ideas, and the Advantage Marketing team will work with you to develop more. After all, helping you write and publish your book is only the beginning if you want it to do the bulk of marketing for your business. We'll help you create a solid plan to ensure your book achieves your goals. Interested? Contact us by visiting advantagefamily.com. Take the first step to more qualified leads for your business and higher income for you.

21
Ways

How to Leverage Your Marketing Dollars

Use a Book to Reach More Prospects and Get a Better Rate of Return

How to Leverage Your Marketing Dollars

Use a Book to Reach More Prospects and Get a Better Rate of Return

Are you paying too much for your marketing and getting mediocre results?

This can be an uncomfortable question for many entrepreneurs and business owners. And many don't *have* an answer. However, I would like your answer to be similar to that of Dr. Scot Gray, who I've introduced in an earlier chapter. He is the chiropractor who uses his book to promote his business. This is how Scot answers this question:

> *"What I love best about having my book is the media attention that it received. I was on NBC, Lifetime Television, and in several newspapers and online sources. This attention alone caused me to get a 3 to 1 return on my investment."*

A 3 to 1 return on his investment from the PR generated due to his book! And this is just *one* of the ways he uses his book for marketing. His ROI does not include the other moneymaking methods such as referrals, lead generation, customer nurturing, or the book as an income stream itself. Are you getting a 3 to 1 return on your marketing or advertising dollars now? Think of the impact on your business if you could get this rate of return, and even *more*.

A book is not only the most powerful marketing tool in an entrepreneur's arsenal, it is often the most cost effective. Why?

To begin, your book is an image booster, business card, direct-response advertisement, and credibility builder *all in one*. Best of all, for less than about $5 per unit, your book does a lot when it comes to marketing. Your book helps people understand what you offer and why you are the better choice. This is *especially* important if you sell a technical or complex product or service. A book is an unparalleled tool to explain why and how your service works. You can also speak directly to the clients you *want* to attract, as Scot does. Your book is a direct marketing tool that generates publicity and builds credibility all at the same time.

A book also allows you to be in multiple places at once, figuratively that is. Think for a minute about the power of multiplicity and leverage. Mass media, for example, allows you to leverage resources. Rather than speaking to people one by one, you can literally speak to thousands, even millions, of people at one time with radio and television. A book allows you to do the same thing.

Speaker, Almon Gunter, knows how well this works. As he says,

> *"When you are a motivational speaker and it is your job to inspire audiences, being a published author validates what they just heard and gives them something tangible to hold onto because I can't be with them 24/7. For me, I speak in front of tens of thousands of people, but through my book, I am able to reach tens of thousands people because they pass it along."*

Eric Pennington is another Advantage author who has experienced this success, especially online. Eric wrote, *Waking Up in Corporate America*, to promote his executive coaching business. He reported that he has "…absolutely been able to use my book as a marketing tool, and in ways that I really did not anticipate. I've had my best success on the Internet, doing virtual book tours or podcasts with bloggers. That has been more effective than my own blog in promoting the book and its ideas."

A book leverages the strengths of people, processes, media, and economies of scale so you can do a lot more in less time. In turn, this helps you to get the most out of *yourself* because you have more free time to work on the activities you value most. This is something Tim Wambach discovered when he worked with Advantage to publish *How*

We Roll. In the book, Tim chronicles his work as a personal aide and caregiver for a young man with Cerebral Palsy, Mike Berkson. Actually, his book is also a story of Mike's sense of humor and awe-inspiring positive attitude.

Advantage author Tim Wambach and friends pose with the inspiration for his book, Mike Berkson, left.

Tim's original goal for the book was to raise awareness for people with special needs. He surpassed this goal beyond his expectations. Tim explains what happened:

> *"With the help and support of Advantage Media Group, we have been able to spread our word to a broad audience. What started as helping Mike has turned into helping others like Mike. We created a foundation, and the 'Keep On Keeping On Foundation' was born."*

This is the *power of leverage* in a book.

However, books have another power that goes well beyond other media and even great examples of direct marketing. This is the power to outlast nearly any other form of messaging. Consider an advertisement on TV or radio. In 30 seconds, it's gone. Trade shows quickly become a distant memory for attendees. Magazines and direct mail are good only until tossed into the recycle bin. Your message within any of these media is like a blip on the radar screen. Here one minute, gone the next.

A book stands the test of time. Our society's reverence for books means we don't throw them away. Instead, we develop libraries, or share our books with others. The result is longevity, for both your book and your message. But for how long?

- Dentist and 3-time Advantage author, Dr. Charles Martin (*How to Build Your Dental Practice with a Book*, *This Won't Hurt A Bit*, and *Are Your Teeth Killing You*), uses TV, radio, and print ads to market his book instead of his practice. He has used this strategy, with an enviable ROI, for more than five years.

- Jim Ziegler wrote his book in 1998. Today it sits on bookshelves in automotive executive offices around the world.

- Carl Sewell has leveraged his book for over 22 years to build an empire of 18 auto dealerships.

Now that's staying power!

If you want to take your business to the next level, you need to work smart, not just hard. After all, when it comes to running a business, small, lean entrepreneurial organizations cannot afford mistakes in marketing. A book allows you to multiply and leverage your marketing, as well as your message and image.

At Advantage, we understand that marketing is the lifeblood of your business, while spending smart is the glue that holds everything together. This is why we offer a range of services at different price levels to help you plan your book, write it, as well as market and monetize it. Find out how we can help put your ideas to print at a price that works for you by contacting us at **advantagefamily.com.**

21
Ways

How to Harness Celebrity Power to Build Your Business

From National TV to Local Radio—Be a Celebrity with Your Book

How to Harness Celebrity Power to Build Your Business

From National TV to Local Radio—Be a Celebrity with Your Book

Have you ever heard of Robert Kiyosaki? What about the book, *Rich Dad, Poor Dad?* If you don't recognize Robert's name, you've probably heard of his book. When Robert launched *Rich Dad, Poor Dad* in 2001, he had already made plenty of money in business and real estate. Yet he was largely an unknown. This book, however, made him a guru in the financial world. He parlayed his newfound fame to make a fortune through speaking, coaching, training, and of course, by writing more books.

A more recent example is Tim Ferris of *The 4-Hour Workweek.* Prior to his book, no one had any clue as to who Tim Ferris was. The book made him famous. Tim has wisely used his fame to his full advantage by commanding high-paying speaking fees and getting top publicity in television, radio, and print. He, too, has gone on to write two more books.

Both of these authors are celebrities. They dominate their respective fields as experts. They have harnessed the celebrity power of a book and gained guru status because of it.

Now, consider Advantage author, Jennifer Nicole Lee. If you watch infomercials or are into fitness, you've likely heard of her. In 1995, Jennifer was a mom of two young boys and she wanted to lose weight. A year later, she was crowned "Miss Bikini America" after losing 70 pounds. Jennifer capitalized on her success and went on to develop a lucrative fitness business.

Fast forward to January 2010. By all accounts, Jennifer had achieved business success. However, she still wanted to share her message and expand her business. For these reasons, she decided to write her first book, *The Mind, Body, & Soul Diet: Your Complete Transformational Guide to Health, Healing, and Happiness*. Jennifer then did what every author should do. She sent copies of her book to manufacturers and publishers in the fitness arena. One of these manufacturers was the maker of Ab Circle Pro. Now, it just so happened at the time, the manufacturer was searching for an Ab Circle Pro spokesperson. They read her book and invited Jennifer for an interview. The rest, as the saying goes, is history. They hired her as their spokesperson, and Jennifer now appears in infomercials around the world.

You can imagine how this has grown Jennifer's celebrity status, business, and income. She receives a royalty for *every* Ab

Circle Pro sold. I think *any* business owner would be excited about results like this.

Advantage author John Patrick Dolan appears as his local news station's legal expert.

Advantage author and lawyer, John Dolan, has leveraged his books to create credibility and expert status with the media. As a result, Fox News, MSNBC, CNN, and local channels regularly interview John about high-profile criminal cases. John recently described how the media introduces him to the TV audience:

> *"The host will say something like, 'John Patrick Dolan, author of* Negotiate Like the Pros *and criminal defense lawyer, is here to talk about the Drew Peterson case.' Then they'll flash a picture of the book. So it's a definite positioning and credibility tool with the media, which then benefits all of my professional pursuits."*

Both John and Jennifer have had outstanding success, and you may be thinking, "These are one-in-a-million results." However, you can be a celebrity *where it counts most*, in your local area, or among your target audience. And when you become that celebrity, you elevate your business above the competition and your income along with it.

Chiropractor, Dr. Leslie Van Romer, is an example of an Advantage author who has created celebrity status on her terms. She has created a reputation as the "community health expert" in her hometown. In fact, a local radio host once introduced her as the "health guru" of the community. All of this is possible because of her book, *Getting Into Your Pants*.

Jim Ziegler, consultant for automotive dealers, is another example. I mentioned how Jim uses his book to generate publicity within this niche. As Jim will tell you, no one knows who he is outside of the automotive industry. But inside this industry, Jim is considered a "rock star." In fact, the president of Ford Motor Company recently flew Jim to Detroit on their corporate jet for a meeting.

This is where being a celebrity really counts: among your audience and in your industry. With a book, you gain ultimate "street credit." You become an authority among prospects and your customers. And for this reason, they buy from you instead of your competition. As author Eric Pennington says, "You don't have to be on Oprah or Dr. Phil for your project to be viable and successful."

At Advantage, we do more than help authors write and publish their books. We work with you to *promote* your book so you can become a celebrity on your terms. Discover how by visiting advantagefamily.com.

21
Ways

Find Prospects Who Are Ready to Buy Without Salespeople

How to Use Your Book to Pre-sell Prospects and Gain New Customers

Find Prospects Who Are Ready to Buy Without Salespeople

How to Use Your Book to Pre-sell Prospects and Gain New Customers

Would you be interested in a proven way to increase sales without adding salespeople to your payroll? Or, put another way, would you like to increase sales without taking extra time to sell?

As an entrepreneur, you know that new customers are your livelihood. And while it would be great to have a dedicated sales force, for most small businesses this just isn't possible. Yet the challenge remains. How do you spread your message and increase sales without the expense of sales staff?

The answer lies in a "virtual sales force," which a book provides at a much lower cost.

With a book, you can be in multiple places at the same time. Here are a few examples:

- I mentioned in a previous chapter how speaker and author, Almon Gunter, reaches thousands of potential customers simply because his book buyers pass copies on to friends and family.
- Dentist, Dr. Charles Martin, gives copies of his book, *The Smart Consumer's Guide to Dentistry*, to all of his referral partners. This includes periodontists, orthodontists, oral surgeons, and other specialists. In turn, they give his book to their patients and leave copies in their waiting rooms.
- Robert Lemon leaves his book with clients and prospects after speaking. He views this as a reference and referral mechanism for future engagements. He is now producing his own television show, with an estimated reach of 20 million viewers. As he says, "This is directly related to the published book and partnership with Advantage Media Group."

A book allows you to multiply yourself, and reach far more people than you have before. This is a definite benefit of your virtual sales force. But there is another.

When readers open your book, it's as if you're sitting across the table. You engage in a personal conversation with them just as a salesperson would. More importantly, when a customer or prospect is reading your book, they are focusing solely on you and your message.

Books allow you to discuss the conflicts and problems your readers face in an open and non-threatening way. You no longer have to make the usual advertising claim that your service is superior to all others. Instead, you hold a conversation with your reader, recognizing their issues, establishing solutions, and showing how your philosophy, service, or product solves their problem. With a book, you create a mindset in your readers. They no longer need your sales message *because they've already bought into it.* After reading your book, they come to you pre-sold and ready to buy.

RICK SESSINGHAUS
Burbank, California

 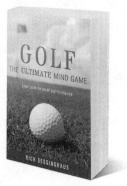

Advantage author, speaker, and golf coach, Rick Sessinghaus, has found that his book, *Golf – The Ultimate Mind Game*, allows him to sell *without actually selling.* Rick explains it this way, "Having a book gets people to start asking me questions instead of me chasing them down. It opens a great line of communication because in the business world, a lot of people play golf and when they see I'm an expert in the field, it helps facilitate communication."

A book is just as important with business-to-business marketing, if not more so, than in the business-to-consumer arena. There are several reasons for this:

- Business products are often technical or complex. A book allows you to explain your system or product in detail. You can educate and entertain your prospects without losing the technical impact. Keep in mind; business buyers are willing to read long copy especially when they work with technical products. They will gladly read books that are relevant and interesting to them.

- In the business world, multiple people are involved in the decision to buy. With a book, you can address everyone's issues and illustrate the benefits they get by working with you. In effect, you can speak to multiple viewpoints in your niche, from controller, to engineer, to company president. Even a one-person shop needs to address all of these issues; they just have to do it *alone*. Your book can provide all the information they need to be comfortable in making a decision.

- Business buying is a multi-step process. There isn't a single marketing piece that wins the sale. It usually takes a series of letters, white papers, emails, brochures, and so on, to convert a lead to a paying customer. Your book is a solid step in building a relationship with your business prospect. It often makes the following marketing steps *easier*—if they are even necessary at all—because your prospect has already bought into your message.

A book is a cost-effective, direct response tool that turns on the spigot of new leads helping you to increase sales without adding overhead and salespeople. Savvy authors also include direct response techniques, bounce-backs, and special offers *within* their book to keep the phone ringing. If you're not sure how to do this, don't worry. We can show you how to make your book a virtual sales force, while keeping your message and philosophies intact. To find out how, contact us at advantagefamily.com.

21
Ways

Are You Reaching Your Target Audience?

How to Cut Through the Noise and
Influence Your Prospects

Are You Reaching Your Target Audience?

How to Cut Through the Noise and Influence Your Prospects

Close your eyes for a moment and picture your top prospect. The CEO of a medium-sized enterprise has just settled into his seat on a flight from JFK to LAX. He rummages through his briefcase to find something to read. Among the papers and folders, his hands land on something solid. It's your book. He thinks to himself, "This is a perfect time to look through this." With that, he opens your book and begins to read. You now have his nearly undivided attention for the next five hours.

As a society, we are overloaded with information from e-mail, TV, radio, and the Internet. With the average American exposed to over 3,000 unique marketing messages every day, having the undivided attention of your prospect or client seems almost impossible.

Fortunately, a book whisks your prospects away from this bombardment of information. They can relax, and enjoy stimulation they simply can't get from other media. Jay Sterling is a professional speaker and Advantage author of *The Other Side of Vision*. I think he summarizes this benefit well:

> *"In the same way that people often prefer reading a book to watching its movie version, a book allows our minds to escape into many arenas that the silver screen can actually limit. Even returning to some of my own writings can sometimes act as a catalyst for new and more creative thinking."*

Better yet, *you* control the conversation and message. Think back for a moment to your prospect, reading your book during his flight. He is giving you his complete attention. Buying this time would be impossible. Even if you had a top-notch salesperson, it would take countless hours and a lot of work just to get a half hour meeting. **With your book, you have jumped to the front of the line and captured his interest.**

This alone makes publishing a book worthwhile. Yet a book cuts through the noise of competition in another way. If you're courting a new potential client, think of how you'll stand out when you send your book. Are you a consultant who's received an RFP? Include your book with your proposal. Perhaps you're a roofing contractor. Imagine how a potential customer will feel when you hand them your book on saving energy in the home. This works for nearly *any* business.

CHRIS RUISI
Newark, New Jersey

This is one reason why executive coach and motivational speaker, Chris Ruisi, published his book. Chris' prospects are CEOs of companies with annual revenues ranging from $40 million to $14 billion. This is not an easy group to break into. However, Chris recently developed a direct mail campaign around his book to reach this target audience. "I'm going to use direct mail because I believe the owners or CEOs of these types of companies are more inclined to read a letter, especially with the book included, than an email from someone they don't know." Several Advantage authors have used similar strategies with great success. Based on their results, Chris' campaign is a sure thing.

Speaker and author, Steve Gilliland, uses his book to make an impression with clients. As a speaker, Steve relies, in part, on speakers bureaus to book appearances. Of course, they receive a portion of his speaking fees for doing this. However, Steve goes a step further. He also pays the bureau a commission for the books sold at the event. As Steve says, "The positive impression I leave on a speakers bureau when our office sends them a commission check for a portion of the product sales from the program is invaluable. It positions me distinctively against other speakers who only generate fee revenue for the bureau." Now consider this from a bureau's point of view. If they have two similar speakers for one booking, whom do you think they'll choose? My bet is on Steve.

Writing a book provides another bonus that many would-be authors haven't considered. As an entrepreneur, you are a visionary. However, communication is the crucial link between vision and execution. Unless you can communicate your vision to investors, employees, and most importantly, to *yourself*, your venture, no matter how inspired, will never succeed. To cut through the clutter, you and your stakeholders must be clear on your vision.

While effective communication requires several components, entrepreneurs should begin with the most critical, which is your message. You must translate your vision into a clear and compelling message and a book is the best medium to do this. Jay Sterling agrees. "Any time you can tailor information to meet the specific needs of your audience, that information obviously becomes more valuable. Writing a book not only forced me to probe and research my material to the nth degree, but also to organize my thoughts and findings into a more cohesive format."

A book connects you with prospects in a way that no other medium can. Your message will be organized with clarity and focus. This catapults you above your competition as never before.

If you have an idea for your book, but don't know where to begin, consider our *Fast Start Author Program*™. With this program, you'll walk away with a complete, organized outline of your ideas, ready for translation to a book. You can stop at this point and simply reap the benefits of organizing your business philosophy and vision. Or, you can continue on to the ultimate benefits of publishing your book. Either way, we can help. Take the first step today by contacting us at advantagefamily.com.

21
Ways

Your Vehicle to Create an Impact While Increasing Your Income

Parlay Your Message into Business Success

Your Vehicle to Create an Impact While Increasing Your Income

Parlay Your Message into Business Success

Let's face it, your message, in the right person's hands, at the right time, can change that person's life. Your knowledge can pull someone out of debt, save a marriage, end someone's pain, or make a difference between a profitable business and bankruptcy. **Whatever your message may be, there are people eager to read it.**

You're in business because you have something unique to share with others, whether it is Stories, Passion, Knowledge, or all three. A book crystallizes this information in one place. It allows you to share your vision on a far-reaching scale. When this happens you not only have opportunities to expand your business, you have opportunities to help others while doing so.

JELYNNE JARDINIANO
New York, New York

Jelynne Jardiniano has experienced this in her business. The young entrepreneur opened her successful restaurant while still in her twenties. Her "ah-ha" moment came when she noticed that people kept asking her for advice on how to start their own restaurant. Following her husband's suggestion, she decided to write *Restaurant from Scratch: How to Trust Your Heart, Listen to the Market, and Beat the Odds.* Since writing the book, she has gone on to other ventures, such as documentary films as well as a food and culture travel show. However, Jelynne's greatest benefit from writing a book was this:

> *"I learned to embrace the message I have to offer and to have faith that my truth will resonate with the people in search of it."*

Psychologist, Linda Hancock, is another Advantage author who is sharing her message while growing her business.

After writing *Life is an Adventure*, Linda secured regular newspaper columns, developed training seminars, and grew a professional speaking business in addition to her regular practice. However, she also achieved her goal of helping others see the potential of living life with an adventurous mindset. In her words, "Because of the treasured place that books have had in my life I have always had a secret desire to become an author who would hopefully influence others." Linda's book has certainly helped her to do this.

Dr. Sonia Kwapisinksi has found that sharing information is one of the greatest benefits in writing a book. By writing *It's Not Your Fault You're Fat*, Sonia was able to share knowledge gained through her personal quest to look and feel better.

> *"I feel compelled to share my knowledge with people who have experienced any health or weight issue. I feel that people are often misinformed and misled in many ways, and through writing on various health topics, I can educate women in such a way that can make them feel much healthier, happier, and in control of their lives."*

When you make an impact with your message, your business seems to expand organically. Teri Johnson is just one of many Advantage authors who find this to be true. As Teri says, "My primary goal was that the message delivered through my book, *Overcoming the Nevers*, would simply impact the life of just one person. That goal was met and exceeded just during the editing process. Doors have opened for me because of the book. Opportunities I never dreamed of are presented to me because I have a book."

Books are the most powerful educational tools in the world because they enable people to share stories and messages that otherwise would not have been possible. Business consultant and author, Eric Pennington, put it this way: "If I knew then (when I began my book) what I know now, I absolutely would have published a book. I had to. The content in the book was inside me and it had to come out."

Now, if you're unsettled by the thought of sharing your vision or writing a book, you're not alone. Many entrepreneurs and business owners feel this way at the start for a variety of reasons. Jelynne experienced these feelings, too. As she says, "Sharing your message with the world, in the form of a book, can be a daunting and intimidating task. It took me three years to complete my book, and Advantage was with me every step of the way. The bottom line is they care; they truly and genuinely care about their authors. And that made all the difference."

Don't let doubt hold you back. Contact us at advantagefamily.com. We will show you how, by sharing your message, you can also grow your business with your book.

21
Ways

The Secret to Creating a Strong, Revenue-Generating Company

Achieve Business Victory by Motivating Employees and Customers

The Secret to Creating a Strong, Revenue-Generating Company

Achieve Business Victory by Motivating Employees and Customers

Why do some companies succeed, while others fail?

Zappos CEO, Tony Hsieh, is qualified to answer this question. When you look back at the company's history, you can see why. Tony joined Zappos at its founding in late 1999 investing $500,000 in the fledgling company. For seven years, he struggled to keep it together and didn't turn a profit until 2007. Yet his employees and customers stuck with him. And in 2009, Amazon purchased the company for *$1.2 billion.*

Of course, Tony worked hard, made sacrifices, and hashed through some tough decisions to achieve this phenomenal success. Still, he triumphed when others, with similar opportunity and resources, crashed. What made the difference?

The difference is Tony's vision, which he communicated with clarity to employees and customers. I think the title of his recent book says it all: *Delivering Happiness – A Path to Profits, Passion, and Purpose.* His vision of customer service and having fun was so clear; he inspired employees to carry it out with passion. Zappos became a family. New customers became repeat customers. They began to spread the word about this customer-centered company. The result was a business that grew exponentially, and continues to grow, in spite of a still shaky economy.

Now, you may not be aiming for Zappos' level of success for your business. But wouldn't it be reassuring to create a business that weathers economic storms and generates income to support the lifestyle you want to have?

You can do this, just as Tony Hsieh has. Strong businesses create a band of people who advocate for you and your company. Employees are inspired, creating a culture around your vision. Customers sing your praises because they believe in your company. In essence, *they do your marketing for you* by spreading the word to friends and through social networks.

Author Steve Gilliland agrees. "For me it is definitely a matter of everyone understanding my vision. My books convey my beliefs and philosophy about how we need to live our lives in order to be happy, content, and contribute to the overall good of the world we share with others. When an employee is on the same page, singing the same song as me, it is easier for them to 'sell' me to a potential client."

The key to achieving this is an inspired vision that you communicate to everyone involved with your company. And the best way to do this is with a book. It doesn't matter whether you have a brand new company, or you've been in business for years. A book sounds your message, inspiring employees who, in turn, cultivate loyal customers.

Great companies are driven by a strong customer-focused architecture and company culture. Their employees share the founder's vision, goals, and strategies. A book is a terrific vehicle to educate your team while creating glue between company and customer. Put your vision to print and share your message with employees and customers. Contact us at advantagefamily.com to get started.

Put your vision to print and share your message with employees and customers.

21 Ways

Be on Par with Industry Giants

How to Level the Playing Field and Rise Above the Competition

Be on Par with Industry Giants

How to Level the Playing Field and Rise Above the Competition

Do you ever feel like a small fish in a big pond? Or do you wonder how you can possibly compete in a big field over-crowded with comparable players?

You're not alone. I think the majority of entrepreneurs and business owners feel this way at one time or another. Yet some have found a way to mix with the big players. They are envied by peers and viewed as experts in fields crowded with specialists. Best of all, they have significantly expanded their businesses in spite of competition.

These business owners are *all* authors. And if you doubt the power of a book to place your business on par with industry giants, consider Jennifer Nicole Lee's story.

I've mentioned in previous chapters how Jennifer built a successful business as a fitness model prior to writing her book. However, since publishing her first book in 2010, she is now a fitness industry icon. By promoting her first book to fitness industry manufacturers, she was hired as a spokesperson for the Ab Circle Pro. From there, she developed a multi-million dollar business, including her own JNL Fusion Exercise DVD program. She has three books on the market now with a fourth in the works. This is what Jennifer has to say about leveling the playing field in her industry:

> *"I've noticed a clear difference in my business before my book, and after. It sets me apart from the pack as far as my credentials. People view me on a higher platform. Even my colleagues, who are in a similar industry yet not authors, really envy my situation. They even look at me as being higher in the ranks of success because I'm a published author."*

If you are going to compete head-to-head with the giants of your industry, you must do so at their level. As an author, you become a member of "the club." Let me explain my point with a story. I often attend the Inc. 500|5000 annual conference and awards ceremony. In fact, Advantage has ranked on the Inc. 500|5000 list of the fastest growing private companies in America. If you're not familiar with Inc., it's a media organization dedicated to helping entrepreneurial businesses, big and small. Their annual conference includes the who's who of industry leaders with an impressive lineup of speakers. At a recent conference, I ran a quick survey to determine how many of the 35 speakers were also published authors. Of the 35 speakers, 27 had written at least one book. Several were CEOs of multi-billion dollar companies.

You can see why being an author positions you in this exclusive group. CEOs of multi-national companies view authorship as being so important, they write their own books. As an author, you join them on the same stage.

Recent Advantage author, Henry Evans, gets this, which is why he is using his book as the foundation for his new information marketing business. For Henry, it all began five years ago, as he built his business by working one hour a day, after his kids were asleep. When he escaped the corporate cubicle three years ago, Henry wanted to help other would-be entrepreneurs to develop their own businesses. He decided that a training program would be the best way to do this. However, Henry also knew that he needed to write a book *first*.

"I want to be able to say I'm a #1 Amazon Best Selling author with this book. That's the credibility piece I need to have for my own info products. There is no question that having a book either puts you on a level playing field with the big players, or gives you an inherent advantage over the small players. That was one of my big reasons for doing a book in the first place."

With that in mind, Henry released *The Hour a Day Entrepreneur – Escape the Rat Race and Enjoy Entrepreneurial Freedom with Only One Focused Hour a Day*, in January 2012. At the time of writing this book, his training academy was set to launch in the fall of the same year. Henry is also ramping up speaking engagements, which, as he says, "The book has definitely helped me with so far." Henry's new business is accelerating, thanks to his book.

Sales coach and speaker, Steve Clark, has unique competition, which his book helps him to rise above. Steve competes against three companies that use books written by authors who have since passed away. Franchisees of each organization still use these books as the basis for their speaking and training. When Steve encounters this competition, he asks this question of his prospects, "Who do you want to work with; the guy who wrote the book, or a speaker who just read someone else's material and is repeating it to you?" Not surprisingly, this consistently tips the scales in Steve's favor. As he says, "It works."

Lawyer, John Patrick Dolan, has leveraged his books to become a giant in his own right in a highly commoditized industry. He is a regular guest commentator on national news channels such as CNN, Fox News, and MNSBC. He is in the top echelon of criminal defense lawyers. He is the Founder and Dean of the new California Desert Trial Academy College of Law. And he is an in-demand and highly paid speaker. John recently described how books allow an author to surpass competition using his speaking business as an example:

"I don't know if you can place a value on the positioning of being the person who wrote the book in the subject

area that you're speaking on, but I can tell you this. In the general speaking marketplace, you have people who speak for honoraria of $500 and you have people speaking for honoraria of $50,000. Most of the time, when you have speakers earning $25,000 to $50,000 they are very well known either because of their publication or their area of expertise. If you look at my Negotiate Like the Pros website, you'll see that I get paid $15,000 to $20,000 to spend between 90 minutes and half a day teaching people about negotiation skills. What I can say is because of having the book and being positioned as an expert, I can command much higher fees than someone who might have the same expertise but doesn't have the publication as evidence of their credibility in their area of expertise."

Now, as a professional, you may also be facing competition from an entrenched institution rather than other industry players. Dr. Scot Gray faces this situation in his chiropractic practice. Scot views his greatest competition not as other chiropractors but as the medical establishment and their use of medications to cover up pain. Scot's book allows him to compete with the pervasiveness of modern medicine, which is an "industry giant" in its own right. Scot puts it this way:

"When people read my book, I tell them why we get back pain and why medicines don't work to end it. I then tell them what chiropractic and natural care is all about. The result

is, I've had patients tell me that after reading my book, they really understand why they need to come in and get adjusted on a regular basis and why their pain never went away. My book helps them to understand what natural health care is all about."

With his book, Scot is leveling the playing field with the medical establishment. New patients rank him alongside, or even above, traditional medicine. And as an added bonus, his book has helped him to rise above the competition of other chiropractors in his city. You can do the same with competition in your profession or industry, whether on a national basis or in your hometown.

SCOT GRAY
Columbus, Ohio

A book will help you create a new business or transform an existing one. It is your ladder to join industry giants on the same stage as well as your tipping point to growth and dramatic profits. If you've thought about writing a book yet hesitate to do so, why not contact us? We will answer your questions and show you how we can help get your book *done* at a price that suits your budget. Your first step to outrunning your competition is here: advantagefamily.com.

21 Ways

Have Plenty of Money to Do What You Want to Do

Achieve Success in Business, Philanthropy, or Both with a Book

Have Plenty of Money to Do What You Want to Do

Achieve Success in Business, Philanthropy, or Both with a Book

Linda Franklin had it all. She was the first Canadian woman to own a seat on the New York Stock Exchange. She also managed an all-male trading department for a leading Wall Street investment firm. Life, as the saying goes, was full.

Then, at the age of 49, Linda walked away from Wall Street. Although she had several solid reasons for leaving, she didn't expect it to be so difficult. After a year of learning not only how to deal with the change, but to thrive in it, Linda decided to write a book, and as Linda says, "… ignite the second act of my life."

I've already mentioned how Linda parlayed her book to create a business and become a spokesperson on issues that affect women over 40. She has also created information products as well as a club where "cougar" women can feel free to network, ask questions, and share ideas.

However, in November 2010, she began to receive emails from women serving in Afghanistan telling her how empowered they felt when reading her blog. Calling themselves "The Combat Cougars," they thanked her for the information and encouragement she was sharing. From that day on, Linda became committed to helping military women. She created Shining Service Worldwide™, a non-profit devoted to recognizing the sacrifice of women in the military and providing services to make their lives a bit easier. Half of Linda's "Real Cougar Woman" website is now devoted to selling products and raising funds for her new charity.

Linda now touches the lives of thousands of women while recreating her life in the process. And it all became possible through her book.

David Johnson is another Advantage author whose book has helped him fulfill his goal of helping others. And interestingly for David, this has strengthened his business. David began his working life as an English teacher and high school tennis coach. However, after spending several summers in international mission work, he left teaching to devote his time to photography. He changed his focus to two major goals: building a freelance business in photography and documenting the human side of the poor and oppressed.

In 2009, he wrote *Voices of Sudan* to share both written and photographic stories of people in Darfur. The book quickly became a conduit for publicity and funding for his non-profit, Silent Images. However, through his book, he has also:

- Increased the number of speaking engagements as well as his fees, and
- Sold "thousands of dollars" worth of prints in addition to the book itself.

However, for David, the most important thing is the money he has raised. He now has more funds than he ever thought possible to provide wells, food, and medicine to residents of Darfur.

Advantage author, David Johnson, with his book, traveling the world.

In addition to all of the above, David has increased his exposure as a photographer and grown his personal photography business as a result. Thanks to his book, he is living his passion through photography while raising awareness and money to help the poor.

Advantage author, Chris Ruisi, furthered his favorite cause when he launched his book, *Step Up and Play Big*. For one set hour during the launch, Chris donated $2.00 from each book sold along with $2.00 of his own funds to the charity Kick Cancer Overboard. Today, he donates 20% of proceeds from his book sales to the Wounded Warrior Project. As he says, "It is a good thing to do, and doing it has given me additional PR." So, in addition to helping two deserving charities, Chris is advancing his business as well.

Linda Franklin, David Johnson, and Chris Ruisi have all used their books to advance a cause while creating or strengthening their business. However, for some Advantage authors, the goal of writing a book was solely to share their message or story so they could help others.

Jimmy Bailey approached his book in this way, although his road to becoming an author was a long one. It began with Jimmy growing up in a working class family in South Carolina. He described himself as a "tough-nosed, rough kid athlete" when he had a chance encounter with a man who would become his mentor. As Jimmy says, "Had it not been for him, I would not be where I am today." From his humble beginnings, Jimmy went on to form a successful business in commercial real estate and to sit in the South Carolina House of Representatives from 1988 to 1994.

However, another chance encounter changed Jimmy's life once again. In November 1998, Jimmy received a copy of a speech, "Solving the Problem of Poverty," written by Steve Mariotti, founder of the nonprofit Network For Teaching

Entrepreneurship (NFTE). The thrust of his speech was that low-income children have an inherent ability to become successful entrepreneurs because of their "street smarts," especially if they have someone to show them the way.

Steve's speech moved Jimmy to his core. He once said, "I thought it was written about Jimmy Bailey and for Jimmy Bailey. I related to it." It was enough to inspire him to action. He, along with several friends, dug deep into their pockets to start Youth Entrepreneurship South Carolina (YEScarolina), a non-profit dedicated to developing the entrepreneurial mindset in South Carolina's youth.

JIMMY BAILEY
Charleston, South Carolina

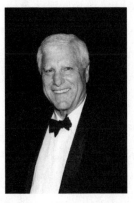

From the very beginning, Jimmy knew he wanted to write a book. His goal was to profile young entrepreneurs so struggling students could see possibilities through their peers. From this idea, *The Spirit of Outreach – 34 Inspiring Stories from YEScarolina* came to be. With this book, Jimmy hopes to "reach kids in a way that we adults can't. It will provide the motivation for them to seek out entrepreneurial courses in their schools, and they end up starting and operating their own business."

Since writing *The Spirit of Outreach*, Jimmy has published a second book, *Teachers Reaching Out – 25 Dedicated Souls Who have Changed the Lives of Young Entrepreneurs*. And today, South Carolina leads the nation in teaching skills that help young people to compete in the new economy.

I'd like to provide you with one more example of how a book can help you to reach your dreams. This story goes back to the time when I first met Tim Wambach, the author who founded the Keep On Keeping On Foundation.

When I first met Tim, he simply wanted to share his experiences working as an aide for a young man with Cerebral Palsy. However, the success of his book inspired Tim, and others, to do more. Today, he is the President of Keep On Keeping On. This charity helps people living with severe physical disabilities as well as their families. Perhaps more importantly, they inspire others to see the disabled person as someone who has a lot to offer rather than as a person in "a chair."

Like the others I've mentioned in this chapter, Tim has parlayed his book into a vehicle for reaching his goals and living his passion. Thanks to the income their books have generated, both directly and indirectly, all of these authors are living life on their terms. If you dream of doing the same thing, we can help. Begin the conversation by contacting us at advantagefamily.com. You'll never know what you can accomplish unless you take this first step.

21 Ways

What Legacy Will You Leave?

How to Make a Lasting Impact Through Your Book

CHAPTER 15

What Legacy Will You Leave?

How to Make a Lasting Impact Through Your Book

How do you want to be remembered?

Will it be for the positive impact you made on the people at your company? Or the help you provided to others in your community? How will your grandchildren or great grandchildren remember you? If you plan to hand your business on to family after you're gone, what will employees and customers know about you and the early years? Will they appreciate the core values and fundamentals on which you built the business?

Only through a book can you record your beliefs, experiences, and history for your family, loved ones, and employees. There will be no debate on what you thought or how you felt. And while it may be somewhat morbid to think about the time after you're gone, this is an important question. **What legacy will you leave behind?**

This is something few authors think about when they decide to write a book. Yet the impact of leaving a legacy often hits home after their books reach an audience. Steve Gilliland experienced this after releasing, *Enjoy the Ride*. In earlier chapters, I mentioned how this book has had a phenomenal impact on Steve's business. As a speaker, he increased his bookings and created a 7-figure annual income. However, Steve has enjoyed another, rather unexpected, benefit. I'll let him tell you how in his own words:

> *"Over the past five years, I have received numerous letters and emails from people who have read* Enjoy the Ride *and commented on how it impacted them. When you receive a letter and someone says it changed their life, it makes you realize that your words can help a person make a single decision that may have a far-reaching effect on generations yet born. There is a fine line between you and hundreds of thousands of lives."*

For Steve, this remarkable benefit was somewhat unexpected. However, Leslie Van Romer knew the implications when she decided to write her book. You may recall that Leslie is the chiropractor who wrote, *Getting Into Your Pants*, to help people lose weight. At first, Leslie did not intend to become an author. However, after working with patients as well as her children, Leslie said:

"Writing a book called to me. Although I tried to ignore the call, ultimately my passion for getting this message out to the world left me with no choice. I started writing. A book is a powerful communication tool, which opens doors and minds, impacts lives, and continues to transmit the message, long after the messenger is gone."

LESLIE VAN ROMER
Greenville, South Carolina

Would you like to leave a message that affects others after you're gone? Even with the numerous business benefits and growth of their income, many Advantage authors view the potential impact of their book as their greatest accomplishment. As Steve Gilliland says, "You never know who may be impacted, and the difference you can make, by the words you speak or write. I am so blessed to have written a couple of books that have impacted a few people along the journey."

You can accomplish the same with your book, leaving a legacy for employees, customers, and most importantly, for your family after you're gone. And it all begins by contacting us at advantagefamily.com.

21
Ways

An Easier Way to Create New Connections and Revenue Streams

Use Your Book to Find Business Partners, Joint Ventures, and New Opportunities

An Easier Way to Create New Connections and Revenue Streams

Use Your Book to Find Business Partners, Joint Ventures, and New Opportunities

Inventor and entrepreneur, Henry Ford, once said, "Take away all of my money and leave me only my rolodex and in one year's time I will be a multi-millionaire all over again." A bold statement? Perhaps. But it certainly illustrates the power of networking. It gives credence to the old saying, "It's not what you know, it's *who* you know."

Networking is essential for most business professionals and even more so for entrepreneurs, business owners, and CEOs. Most will agree; networking develops relationships that result in business ventures. In spite of this, many people feel that networking is costly or takes too much time and effort. And they can be right, especially if you go about it in the traditional way.

However, a book provides you with a networking shortcut. A book allows you to declare your business philosophies and solutions to specific problems. You have the ability to link with people who share your beliefs or need your answers. And some of these people will view you as an ally or potential business partner. You are now able to network with people who are *predisposed* to doing business with you. This is your key to making networking easier and far more profitable.

This is exactly what happened for Rick Sessinghaus, the golf pro and coach who wrote *Golf – The Ultimate Mind Game*. Rick does everything right when it comes to using his book to build his business. And the same applies to his networking. As he recently told me, "I've had some great things happen by my book getting in the right person's hands."

Rick's book allowed him to solidify a relationship with *Golf Tips Magazine* where he is now a member of the contributing editorial staff. They also feature his book in the magazine as well as on their website. In addition, the book opened the lines of communication with select golf facilities and franchises located in more than 100 cities nationwide. Rick reports that he now speaks at some of their sites, *every month*, and his book was "the initial door opener."

Steve Sax calls his book "a connector for new business." I mentioned in an earlier chapter that Steve is a retired baseball player who now has a coaching and speaking business aimed at professionals and companies. However, after reading his book, people have hired Steve to run baseball clinics. This is something he never anticipated in his business model. However, it has been a fun way for him to earn extra money.

Brian Fricke's book, *Worry Free Retirement*, brought him an unexpected business deal. An ad agency specializing in marketing and promoting senior retirement communities found Brian on the Internet, thanks to his book's title. They hired him as a guest speaker because they felt his topic would attract potential buyers and tenants. As Brian says, "They were using me as their lead generator."

However, this opened Brian's eyes to new business opportunities. He is now in the process of sending marketing materials to agencies that cater to developers of retirement communities across the country. Brian admits this was "totally off my radar. However, it got me thinking about other industries that market to the same ideal client that we do. Will they find it attractive to hire me as a speaker and give my book to their customer base, and in essence, pay me to do my own lead generation?" Not surprisingly, Brian is exploring possibilities in this area.

Sometimes just the process of writing a book connects you with the right people. Bryan Crabtree co-authored *The Advantage of Real Estate* with 11 other prominent real estate professionals located throughout the country. Because of networking made possible just by writing the book, Bryan met several investors. He decided to purchase a property with one of his new colleagues. If all goes as planned, these two investors will flip the property for a healthy profit. That one deal alone could result in thousands of dollars for Bryan's bank account – a deal made possible by networking generated from his book.

A book is your introduction to like-minded people and organizations. It opens the door to new spheres of influence often in surprising ways. Tara Kennedy-Kline found this to be true after writing her book on coping with her son's Asperger's Syndrome. I've cited in earlier chapters how Tara has grown her business and non-profit organization through her book. However, Tara describes her greatest benefit this way:

"I think the biggest thing that has happened, as a result of all of this, is the connections that I've made as a result of just having written the book. I've met so many amazing people and those things have turned into bigger things, bigger networking opportunities and helping more people, which is really amazing. That has been transformational for me."

There are partnerships and opportunities waiting for you that you have likely never thought of. A book connects you to people who *want* to work with you, rather than you having to hunt for people as you do with traditional networking.

Jennifer Nicole Lee also experienced this first hand. In one of her books, she sang the praises of Endermologie equipment, which tightens skin and reduces cellulite. Well, it happened that an intern working at Daniele Henkel in Canada read her book and passed it on to the company's CEO. The serendipity here is this company is the worldwide distributor of Endermologie. The company wasted no time in asking Jennifer to be their US Ambassador. They also partnered with her to open the new JNL Beauty and Wellness center in Coral Gables, Florida.

Three-time Advantage author, Jennifer Nicole Lee, poses with the many magazine covers she's appeared in as a celebrity fitness model and spokesperson.

And all of this became possible because, as Jennifer said:

"I mentioned one of my beauty secrets in my book. You have to make the investment of a book in your company and yourself. I did and it has brought me countless opportunities, speaking engagements, and business ventures that have been very lucrative for me."

It's *your* turn to open doors to new business partnerships, joint ventures, affiliates, *and new income*. When you contact us by visiting advantagefamily.com, we'll show you how you can write a book that will create these opportunities for your business.

21
Ways

Everything You Need On a Business Card and More

Give Prospects Your Contact Information and Unique Selling Proposition with Your Book

Everything You Need On a Business Card and More

Give Prospects Your Contact Information and Unique Selling Proposition with Your Book

Picture yourself meeting with a prospective client. You shake hands and sit down. In the past, you would have slid your business card across the table. But today, you reach into your briefcase and pull out your book.

You tell your prospect, "Thank you so much for spending a few minutes with me today. I greatly appreciate your making time to meet with me. As a small token of my appreciation, I would like you to have an autographed copy of my latest book. I think you will find the information I've provided to be very useful."

A familiar scenario now has a very different outcome. You have become more than another salesperson with a pitch.

You are an author, an expert in your particular subject. Whereas your prospect may have initially viewed her time with you as a "favor," you suddenly become the expert that is there to help. As Advantage author and world-renowned marketing guru, Dan Kennedy, likes to say, "In the mind of your prospect, with a book you go from being an *unwanted pest* to a *welcomed guest*."

DAN KENNEDY
Cleveland, Ohio

Advantage author, Burrow Hill, finds his book makes it easier to reach prospects. "My book has opened doors and started so many conversations for me. Using the book as my business card is certainly the fastest way to get past a gate-keeper to the decision maker for me."

Rick Sessinghaus, the golf pro and author that I've introduced in previous chapters, also has great success using his book as a business card. Like many speakers, Rick prepares speaker packets to encourage bookings. However, Rick includes his book with his speaker packet. He tells how this makes a difference for his business:

"So, if I'm giving my speaker packet to a CEO of a company, they get my book with it. Maybe they're going to throw the packet in the filing cabinet, but they're probably going to keep that book out either for themselves or to give to someone they know who plays golf. My face is on the back of the book. Of course, my name is on the front and my website is on the back, too. It's used as the ultimate business card for a lot of things. It helps with credibility and, of course, getting people to visit my website."

Financial planner and author, Brian Fricke, carries business cards but he rarely hands them out. If someone asks for his card Brian will say, "I just gave my last business card away. Why don't you give me your card? I'd like to send you a copy of my book and add you to my newsletter list." This is a very smart strategy to promote his business and build his list at the same time.

Like Brian, coach and speaker, Steve Clark, carries copies of his book in his briefcase. "When someone asks me for a business card, I like to reach into my briefcase and say, 'I don't have a business card but would you like an autographed copy of my book?' That really does get their attention."

There are several ways you can use your book as a business card. You can...

- Take it to prospect meetings, as I described in the opening.
- Include it in speaker packages, as Rick does.
- Enclose it in your proposals or in your "shock and awe" packages.
- Send it to potential, high-caliber prospects as the ultimate introduction to your services.

Advantage author and speaker, Almon Gunter, also uses his book as a business card but in a rather unique way. He carries books with him whenever he travels. If he meets interesting people, he gives them an autographed copy. I like the story that Almon recently shared with us.

"I met an 18 year old in the military on his way to Iraq. I autographed a book and gave it to him. I think everyone on the plane saw my book before they got off. As you can imagine, giving a book is far more powerful than a business card."

You can never predict who might find or read your book. One of these people could be a future customer. And after reading your book, they will be pre-sold on your company even before they meet you or visit your website. This is why we ensure that every book we publish has all of your contact information for you and your business. Some will argue that your contact information page is the *most* important one in your book.

Visit advantagefamily.com to get started on exploring how you can write and publish your book. We ensure that our authors have everything they need to make their book the "ultimate" business card. Rather than sliding your card across the table, start sliding your book instead. Then watch for the amazing changes in *your* business.

CHAPTER 18

21
Ways

Motivated Customers Who Buy and Reduced Competition

How to Create a Brand that People Recognize and Value

Motivated Customers Who Buy and Reduced Competition

How to Create a Brand that People Recognize and Value

As a young entrepreneur, I am interested in reading anything on building and operating a successful company. So, naturally I read, *Pour Your Heart Into It: How Starbucks Built a Company One Cup at a Time,* written by Starbuck's Chairman and CEO, Howard Schultz.

Prior to reading this book, I had never stepped foot in a Starbucks, mainly, because I don't drink coffee. However, after finishing it, I gained a real appreciation for Starbucks' corporate values and the way they treat employees, vendors, and suppliers. So much so, I became a regular customer. If I'm given a choice of coffee and tea outlets to choose from, I will definitely pick Starbucks. I'll even go out of my way to walk to one. And my loyalty came to be because I read the CEO's book.

Do you think the CEO of Starbucks wrote his book as a networking tool or as a business card? Probably not. But Howard Schultz did write the book to create goodwill for the Starbucks brand and to drive new people into the stores. It worked with me. And it likely had something to do with Starbucks' meteoric growth. When Schultz published his book in 1999, Starbucks had 2,500 store locations. As of June 2012, Starbucks had 19,763 outlets in 59 countries.

A book will help you to build brand recognition in your niche or industry. It can also put you on equal footing with big players. Author and businesswoman, Jennifer Nicole Lee, has amplified both her brand and her business after publishing three books. I've mentioned how Jennifer is now the spokesperson for Ab Circle Pro. She accomplished this, in large part, because she sent her first book to the Ab Circle Pro manufacturers.

Jennifer's brand *is* Jennifer Nicole Lee. Although well known in certain fitness circles, these infomercials have made her a widely recognizable star. She grabbed this fame and ran with it creating more products and developing new business partnerships.

Steve Gilliland's first book skyrocketed his brand to new heights, almost overnight. Steve is another Advantage author who uses books to create remarkable growth in his business. I told you earlier how Steve doubled his speaking engagements in the year following the release of his first book, *Enjoy the*

Ride. I think this story from Steve really illustrates how his book also increased his brand recognition:

> *"Maybe the most gratifying thing about publishing a book is the encounters I have had with people who have read my book. My most unforgettable experience was boarding a flight in Chicago. Just after our departure, I noticed the flight attendant was reading* Enjoy the Ride. *After frequent looks of inquisitiveness, she finally realized that I was the author and was delighted when I obliged her request to autograph her book. What astounded her most was that she had purchased the book at Hudson Booksellers in O'Hare Airport just moments before boarding the plane—and there I was on her flight."*

Imagine. You're recognized on a flight because someone is reading your book. While this may not happen often, Advantage authors *are* celebrities within their industry or niche markets, thanks to their books. They stand out, and become the company of choice, even among tough competition.

This is certainly the case for Advantage author, Peter Turpel, President and CEO of Phone On-Hold Marketing Systems Inc. Peter has experienced interesting results in branding his company:

> *"I am the first published author in my industry. I wasn't looking for a best seller, but for a book that I could share*

with my prospects and clients. With my book, prospects truly understand the value and importance of what our industry provides. The book certainly brands my company as 'the expert' and differentiates us from all competitors. The publishing of this book has done that and more, to not only my clients, but my competitors, as well. As a matter of fact, I have a competitor that buys my book on Amazon and makes it required reading for his new salespeople."

PETER TURPEL
Glendale, California

Now that is a unique outcome: a competitor buys your book to train his staff. Thanks to his book, Pete's company definitely has the "expert" brand.

Now if you're thinking that branding is important only for professionals and business owners, I'd like to share John Wood's story. John is the founder of Room to Read, a non-profit organization that builds libraries for children in third world countries. Like most of us, John has a fascinating personal story. However, he decided to share his story in a book, *Leaving Microsoft to Change the World*.

Not long ago, a friend recommended that I read John's book. After reading it, I was so excited about Room to Read that I immediately made a financial contribution. Since then, thousands of other readers have had the same positive reaction. John's book has brought a flood of new volunteers and contributors to his charitable organization.

You, too, can leverage your book to build brand recognition and equity for your company or your cause. However, it's important that you write, publish, and market your book with this in mind. Our goal at Advantage is to help you do this. After all, your book *should* make your marketing more effective, so you stand above your competition. Discover how we can help you build brand recognition through your book by visiting advantagefamily.com.

21
Ways

Create Your Own Money Printing Machine

How to Use a Book to Acquire Leads and Build Your List

Create Your Own Money Printing Machine

How to Use a Book to Acquire Leads and Build Your List

Many years back, my friend, colleague, and Advantage author, Tom Antion, and I were having a conversation about Internet marketing when he asked me a question that forever changed my life.

His question was, "Do you know what your computer is?" After staring back at him with some confusion, he stated, "Your computer is an ATM where you can instantly print money whenever you need it."

Tom's point applies to any business owner, entrepreneur, or professional. By building a large list of prospects and customers, you can communicate with them at any time. If you create a community that knows and trusts you, they will respond when you offer something of value. This translates to sales. In fact, Tom's list of 110,000 customers, prospects, and subscribers generates from $90,000 to $200,000 *every* month!

I've never forgotten Tom's lesson, and frankly, neither should you. If you were to pull in 10%, even 1%, of Tom's monthly income from your list, think of how this money would help your business. At the lowest amount, this would still be $900 in extra cash every month. **With an active list, you *can* create new income streams. And a book is one of the best ways to accomplish this**.

Dan Kennedy, marketing guru and Advantage author, is a master at using his books to build lists. You may be aware of Dan's *No B.S.* books. I hope you've read at least one because they are all written to help entrepreneurs and business owners make more money. If you haven't picked up a Dan Kennedy book yet, I suggest you do. There are several to choose from on Amazon or any online bookstore.

Within the first 10 to 15 pages of any Dan Kennedy book, you will find a free resource offer that drives you to a website. Here, you enter your contact information in exchange for something of value such as a free report, article, or teleseminar. Dan subtly weaves these free resources (aka offers to join his "list") throughout his books. And there is a sound marketing strategy for doing this.

When you sell your books or give them away, you never know where they will land. When people buy your book on Amazon, they are *not* your customers. They are Amazon's customers. Unless you have a way to entice them to visit your website, or to request more information, you will never know who they are. And you lose potential customers as well as new revenues.

Like Dan, you should pepper offers throughout your book, directing readers to get something valuable from your website. You want them to "raise their hand" and say, "YES, I want to hear from you, I want to learn more, I want you to stay in contact with me."

Several Advantage authors have done this, many in creative ways. After releasing his book, *Engagement is Not Enough*, Keith Ayers offered a free subscription to *Weekly Leadership Tips* on his website. The tips take only two to three minutes to read and are easy to implement. Of course, they come directly from his book. Keith refers to the book at the end of each tip and provides a link where the reader can buy it. He also gives his subscribers an easy way to forward the tip to someone else thus building his list through sharing.

Steve Clark created a landing page with a URL that matches the title of his book, *Profitable Persuasion*. He regularly directs people to this site where they can download a *free* copy of his book in exchange for their contact information.

This is a strategic move on Steve's part. His book attracts new prospects at the top of his lead funnel. People read his book and get excited about the possibilities of selling more products, faster. However, as it is with many people after reading a book, they have questions. Many want more information or step-by-step guidance. They are willing to purchase more in-depth information and assistance. By giving his book away, Steve is losing some income now. However, he is gaining a deep pool of prospects for future products and sales. **His strategy will bring in a lot more money over the long run.**

Fitness model and author, Jennifer Nicole Lee, has a creative way to attract new subscribers through her YouTube channel, *Jennifer Nicole Lee Worldwide*. She occasionally holds drawings for autographed copies of her book. To enter, viewers must sign up on her website. Jennifer has had tremendous success in building her list this way. And, since she has three books, she can create a variety of offers that appeal to different people. Some want her fitness book, while others sign up to win her cookbook. This allows her to add even *more* names to her list.

HENRY EVANS
San Diego, California

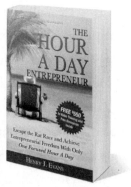

Henry Evans, author of *The Hour a Day Entrepreneur,* reports that he has not only grown his list, he has "broadened" it as well. Henry's list used to include residents from San

Diego, California where he lives and works. Six months after writing his book, Henry had subscribers from across the U.S. and as far away as Japan.

Don't let new prospects, customers, or clients slip through your fingers. Help them to discover you through your book. Engage them with irresistible offers, and drive them to your website. Watch your list grow along with your opportunities to make money. At Advantage, we will help you write a book that *works* for your business. Join the hundreds of Advantage authors who are generating more money, thanks to their books. Get started by contacting us at advantagefamily.com.

21 Ways

Secrets of Highly Paid Speakers

How to Be In Demand, Command Higher Fees, and Enjoy Motivated Audiences

CHAPTER 20

Secrets of Highly Paid Speakers

How to Be In Demand, Command Higher Fees, and Enjoy Motivated Audiences

Speaker, Steve Gilliland, doubled his bookings in the first year after publishing his book. Yet he almost didn't publish it.

Steve reported that he came close to ending his work on *Enjoy the Ride* halfway through the project.

> "My speaking business was growing and I wasn't convinced a book would make it that much better. Added to the fact that I didn't have a lot of extra money to invest in the project, it should readily become apparent why I wanted to quit. I started to write less and less every day until I remembered what a former coach had said to me. 'Nothing is more important than the score at halftime. You will always ease off when you lack understanding and you will always quit when you lack faith.' And with that reminder, I borrowed

some strength from my past, stopped thinking about the way things are, and started focusing on what I wanted them to be. I wanted a book to compliment my speaking career, so I continued writing and never looked back again."

Was it worth it? I'll let Steve share his amazing statistics.

"From 1999 to 2006, I typically spoke before audiences, large and small, 75 times each year, without having published a book. The year after Advantage Media Group released my first book, Enjoy the Ride, *my bookings surged. I immediately gained credibility and increased my marketability within months of its release. By 2008, I was averaging 150 speaking engagements annually!"*

In addition to increased bookings, Advantage authors also enjoy higher speaking fees. John Dolan receives $15,000 to $20,000 for his half-day seminars. Steve Sax reports, "My book has enhanced my speaking fees by 30 to 50%. Add to that the passive income that I generate when I sell my books at the back of the room and it definitely is a help to my business."

All of these authors will tell any speaker that writing a book is an absolute must. Steve Gilliland says, "I am now an advocate for speakers who don't have a book to write one." The reason for this is simple. A book is the secret to financial success. And Steve has gone beyond using his book just to promote speaking engagements. Like many Advantage authors, he has parlayed his book to create a seven-figure income.

Whether you're a seasoned, professional speaker or just starting out, writing a book will jumpstart any speaking business. Greg Kozera, Advantage author of *Learned Leadership*, is a motivational leadership speaker for high school students as well as industry professionals. Yet he does this in addition to his job managing a regional sales team for an engineering firm. After publishing his book, Greg was able to secure more bookings all while substantially increasing his speaking fee. Greg's book helped him to earn a healthy six figures in speaking fees in a little less than a year. Keep in mind; he does this on a *part-time* basis.

As Steve Gilliland mentioned, being an author increases your credibility almost instantly. Your book shows a meeting planner or speakers bureau that you are an authority on your topic. They have a clear outline of the information you'll cover *before* they hire you. You are a safe bet for a successful event, something that any meeting planner or booking agent wants to ensure.

Motivational speaker, Jay Sterling, knows this first hand. He agrees that most organizations want, at the very least, an outline of the topics he plans to cover. He tells a story of a time, before publishing his book, when he was booked to speak at an international business conference. The group of executives planning the event wanted to ensure that Jay's topic was appropriate for their critical audience. They were so concerned, Jay had to provide his entire speech in writing before the event. As he said, "If my book had been written at the time, I could have simply handed them a copy and saved myself a lot of anguish!"

ALMON GUNTER
Jacksonville, Florida

Your book also gives you flexibility to secure speaking engagements with organizations that cannot afford your fee. Speaker and author, Almon Gunter, uses this strategy with great success. If an organization is unable to cover his fee, he will suggest they buy some of his books instead. If they purchase a certain minimum number, he doesn't charge a speaking fee at all.

This is a very smart tactic. Some organizations simply do not have budgets for speaking fees. However, they do have budgets for educational materials. Books fit this category perfectly. In fact, I would argue that you're getting a much better deal than an outright fee. When you're finished speaking, your book will be in the hands of 50, 100, or even more people. They will read it and pass it on to friends and colleagues. You gain a much larger audience than you would have by simply speaking to the group.

Jay Sterling maintains that writing a book has another important benefit for any professional speaker. He believes it makes you stronger on stage. Here's why:

"As a speaker, I was often advised that writing a book could elevate my credibility, strengthen my brand, and serve as a powerful marketing tool. And while I am genuinely convinced that all of these things are true, I am equally surprised to learn that writing a book has also improved my capabilities on the speaker's platform. Now, rather than resorting to my methodical script that represents years of an all too familiar comfort zone, I can easily integrate a variety of new material into my live presentations by merely perusing the subchapters of my book. A quick glance reminds me of the many important subtleties that I labored over in wanting my key points to be understood in their written form. I knew they'd work in presentations as well."

Like many authors, Jay finds that his book also "creates an unspoken excitement and intrigue" before he even steps on stage. Books not only serve as a tease for the live presentation, they offer an extension of the information and experience you've shared after your event is over.

This effect works for both Advantage authors who speak professionally as well as those who speak primarily to market their principal business. Dr. Scot Gray became a speaker after releasing his book, in part because he enjoys it, but also because it is so effective in securing new patients for his practice.

Unlike professional speakers, Scot does not work with speakers bureaus or event planners. He approaches companies, hospitals, and community groups on his own. His book makes it easy to contact these organizations because he has a "reason why" they should listen to him. "I tell them my book teaches people how to eliminate pain and have better quality of life and that I want to share these principles. It's a far better approach than just saying I want to talk to people about back pain." His method certainly works since he usually speaks once every week.

Scot typically provides lectures at no cost to the organization. In fact, he offers his book as a free bonus for people when they attend. He has found that "people like books, so they often come to my talk primarily to get my book." In addition, his book provides the "credibility that many people need before they will work with you." It has been so successful for him; he typically recruits at least one new patient at every speaking session. This is big money for Scot. On average, one patient generates $1,200 to $1,500 per year. At one person per week, multiplied by $1,200 or $1,500 over 52 weeks, this translates into $62,400 to $78,000 in new annual income. Not a bad way to build a profitable practice!

Being an author and speaking go hand in hand. If you're a professional speaker, your career will be boosted with a book. If you own a business or professional practice, you have an easy way to market and build your business at the same time.

Your book will open the door to speaking, or crank up your speaking business, almost instantly. I would be happy to tell you more, but you need to take the first step by contacting us at advantagefamily.com. Don't hesitate. As Jay Sterling says, "A book will continue to pay great dividends in ways you have yet to discover."

21 Ways

The Secret to Creating Multiple Revenue Streams in Your Business

How to Generate New Business with a Book

The Secret to Creating Multiple Revenue Streams in Your Business

How to Generate New Business with a Book

Can you imagine making $1,000 from a book that sells for $20? What about 100 times that amount?

If you think this is impossible, consider this. Several Advantage authors achieve this now. In fact, they have multiplied revenues from their books into six or seven-figure incomes. So, how do they do it?

These authors turn their books into audio books, home study kits, teleseminars, coaching programs, and material for high-end consulting that can easily generate this type of income. **Their books become the foundation for lucrative information businesses.**

I've introduced Rick Sessinghaus in earlier chapters. You may recall that he is a golf pro who uses his book to increase his speaking and coaching bookings. Just by doing this, his book has helped him to grow his business at a phenomenal clip. Rick could have stopped here, yet he's using his book to develop even more revenue streams.

"I am now using my book in leveraging my database more and earning money on that end by turning the book into an audio program and using that material for other workshops. The book is really going to spawn off into a lot of other products."

Speaker Steve Gilliland is another Advantage author you've met in previous chapters. Like Rick, Steve's first book made an incredible impact on his business. As he says, "My revenues absolutely and unequivocally eclipsed the one million dollar mark on the speaking side of my business after my first book."

Steve could have been satisfied with this growth in his business. However, he has also produced several spin-off products from his books. All of his books are now for sale in audio format. He sells CDs of his presentations with the same title as his book, *Enjoy the Ride*, which as Steve notes, "lends itself to more exposure and marketing opportunities." Plus, he offers DVDs of his presentations. In addition to selling the DVDs on their own, he cross promotes his book by offering a copy when customers purchase the DVD.

This has been so successful that within two years of releasing his first book, he opened a new division in his company. This division handles the development, administration, and distribution of his products. He now has two offices in two locations: his product division located in Freeport, Pennsylvania and his speaking home base in Mocksville, North Carolina. Steve is also working with Advantage now to develop more information marketing products.

I've told you how speaker and marketer Tom Antion uses his books to build his list. He is also brilliant at tapping into books to develop products. Tom's 326-page book, *Wake 'Em Up! Business Presentations*, sells for $24.95. Each of its 20 chapters highlights a different strategy to engage people in your presentation. Being the KING of product development, Tom turned his book into CDs and interactive learning kits. By expanding on different topics and developing CDs, Tom has several products ranging in price from $29.95 to $97.00.

However, Tom went a step further. Tom combined his book with additional information to create the *Wake 'Em Up Speakers System*. Today, he sells this system for $1,597.00. Tom has easily sold over $1 million dollars worth of his Speakers System. And it all began with his original $25 *Wake 'Em Up!* book.

I'd like to provide one more example with Advantage author, Ron Seaver. Ron had a solid, 25-year business in connecting corporate sponsors with sports organizations and athletes. However, he believes that sponsorship opportunities are also available for speakers, authors, and information marketers. To that end, Ron wrote his first book, *Getting Yourself Sponsored – For Authors, Associations, or Any Business – Your Blueprint to Unlock Brand New Revenue Streams*. From here, he developed his *Brought to You By – The Ultimate Sponsorship Sales System*, which includes several manuals, CDs, checklists, and DVDs. Today, Ron sells this system for $2,497.00. He also offers monthly coaching calls where he provides news and tips, and answers questions. This membership retails for $47 each month. And Ron now offers an annual Sponsorship Bootcamp with different price points for new attendees as well as Bootcamp alumni.

Advantage author, Ron Seaver, creates additional revenue streams through his Sponsorship Bootcamp.

It's interesting to note that Ron continues to offer his book at a low cost on his website. By providing easily accessible copies of his book, Ron gets people interested and engaged. He builds rapport and demonstrates the value he provides. He then moves prospects down his funnel to higher priced items. With this system, Ron has built a lucrative information marketing business. Once developed, many of his products require little time and input from him. His *Brought to You By* system rolls in the money with virtually no additional effort. Plus, it keeps customers coming back for more, higher-ticket services.

Author Henry Evans is very blunt about using his book to develop his information marketing business. Although he will generate income by selling his book, his goal for it is lead generation. Henry recently said, "I look at it more as a lead generating, front-end tool to get people into my marketing funnel."

You may decide to write a book to share your business message then develop information products as Steve Gilliland and Tom Antion have. Or, you may follow in the footsteps of Ron Seaver and Henry Evans by starting a new information marketing business with your book. Either way, **you have tremendous opportunities to create new revenue streams that flow money into your business, even while you sleep!**

Think of what you could do with the additional income information products can provide. We can help you achieve this with your current book or with the book you dream of writing. With our *Monetize Your Book*™ online learning system, our experts will turn your content into online courses—*your* first step in building your own information marketing empire. Find out how we can help by contacting us at advantagefamily.com. There is money ready to be made! Get started by contacting us now.

21 Ways

How to Write a Book —Quickly and Easily—On a Businessperson's Schedule

You Can Be a Published Author Even if You're Not a "Born Writer"

CHAPTER 22

How to Write a Book — Quickly and Easily — On a Businessperson's Schedule

You Can Be a Published Author Even if You're Not a "Born Writer"

In 2011, Thomas Helbig was a busy, "struggling" financial planner in St. Louis, Missouri. Like many entrepreneurs, his days were crammed with client meetings, phone calls, and follow-up. He had to keep track of Wall Street, new regulations, an office, and staff. And if this wasn't enough, he was trying to promote his business in a commoditized industry where financial planners are found on nearly every street corner.

Today, Thomas is still a busy financial planner. However, he is now a bestselling author. Within months of publishing his book, his credibility as a financial planner soared. He is now taking on "only the more valuable clients." Profits continue to climb. Best of all, he is no longer struggling.

Thomas set a new course for his business, thanks to a book that he wrote and published in the span of six months And he accomplished this with little impact on his day-to-day activities—or his spare time.

So how did he do it?

Thomas literally *talked* his way through his book, thanks to Advantage Media Group's renowned *Talk Your Book*™ program.

THOMAS HELBIG
Saint Louis, Missouri

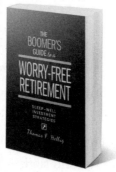

Talk Your Book™ is a practical approach to authoring that has revolutionized book publishing for busy professionals and business owners. In addition to saving valuable time, it plays to your strengths, even when writing feels like a chore or you don't know where to begin.

This is why Thomas chose to "talk" his book. He recently told me, "I didn't know where to start; I'm not a born writer. Advantage said if I have a seminar, I could speak it and they could turn that into a manuscript. I do this seminar every month and I know the subject so well, it made sense."

For some authors, the program helps them to overcome personal obstacles that make writing difficult. This was the case for Tara Kennedy-Kline, who faces the challenge of ADD. *Talk Your Book* made it possible to achieve her dream of being an author. "Because of the whole ADD thing, what I realized was the *Talk Your Book* program that Advantage offers was absolutely necessary for me. I felt like I was part of a bigger picture. I was part of a family rather than just this person that wrote a book."

***Talk Your Book* works because you control your message while an Advantage editor puts it into the written word.** We make it a point to choose an editor with a background that works for your business and your ideas. Your book then begins to take shape with an outline that you help create.

Now comes the time to get your message on paper with this easy option. You will talk your book in a series of recorded phone calls. During each call, you simply talk about your business, message, and ideas using your outline as a guide.

Your editor will harvest and edit the resulting transcripts. These eventually become your first rough draft. You'll then have several opportunities to edit your book, making sure it says what you want it to say as perfectly as possible. From here, you collaborate with our graphics experts to develop a cover design and interior layout. Finally, after we have your stamp of approval, your book goes to press. Before you know it, copies will arrive at your door.

However, our support doesn't end after we ship your books. At Advantage Media Group, we recognize that our success is based on your success. This is why we continue to provide support, advice, and ongoing programs to help you reach your goals, long after your book is published. Most of our authors find this to be as important as the process of publishing itself. Teri Johnson described her experience this way:

"From the very beginning, from flushing out the ideas, and brainstorming with the team, writing the outline and talking the book—through to the day the actual book was personally delivered to my hands and after—working with the Advantage team, the experience was and is positive, encouraging, and enjoyable."

Jim Serger, author of *Go the Distance*, echoed Teri's comments when he told me:

"Being a first time writer, and not knowing what is around the corner can be a nerve wracking situation, but your team set my mind at ease. Yes, I did call a lot and, without any hesitation at all, your staff answered all the questions I had—and still do to this day. I can pick up the phone and still feel as connected as I did on my first phone call."

A book is the ultimate game-changer for your business. Advantage authors leverage their books to exponentially grow their businesses—and their incomes. This is why they will tell you to do whatever it takes to publish yours. As Peter Turpel says, "For many years, I wanted to write a book, and never seemed to find the time. With the *Talk Your Book* program, I was able to achieve that wish and be the first published author in my industry."

They will also tell you it's one of the best—if not *the* best—investments they've made in their business. Yes, it takes some time and money, but author, Burrow Hill, summed it this way:

"As a numbers guy, I found working with Advantage to be less expensive than any other means. When I placed the appropriate hourly rate on my time and added up the time it would have cost me to: research, get proposals, evaluate and hire a self-publisher; research, get proposals, evaluate and hire editors, designers, photographers, cover designers, etc., it was less expensive, faster, and dramatically easier to use Advantage."

And I should add, Burrow now calls his book "the cornerstone" of his business.

Contact us today at 866.775.1696 or advantagefamily.com. We'll answer any questions you have about timing, investment, and the many options available to make your book a reality. And if you're still hesitating, consider this advice from three-time Advantage author and international fitness celebrity, Jennifer Nicole Lee:

> *"The opportunities are endless with a book. The Talk Your Book program really helped me. It helps anyone who has difficulty writing or has little time. There are endless opportunities when you work with Advantage Media Group and I am very proud to be part of the Advantage Family."*

If you too are an ADD entrepreneur and the thought of sitting down and writing a book makes your head spin, perhaps the *Talk Your Book* program is perfect for you. Give us a shout at 866.775.1696 or visit advantagefamily.com to request a complimentary Discovery Call with an Acquisitions Editor.

Are You Ready to Achieve More than You Ever Thought Possible?

A book is your game changer. It's the missing link you need to accelerate your business, communicate your message, and reach your dreams.

Success from your book begins with a strong strategy, develops with experienced editing, grows with sound marketing, and takes flight with a monetization plan. At Advantage, we can help you with one or all of these steps, depending on where you are in the process. You'll be an author with a professionally published book that imparts *your* message to your audience.

ARE YOU TAKING THE FIRST STEP? NOT SURE WHERE TO BEGIN?

With our *Fast Start Author Program*™, we'll help you develop your book strategy and editorial outline. You'll walk away with a blueprint unique to you and your business. From here, you decide on your next step, whether it's publishing with us or creating it on your own. Whatever you decide, the insight you will glean from this process will be invaluable to you even if you *never* write a book.

DO YOU SEE A BOOK IN YOUR FUTURE BUT WORRY ABOUT THE TIME IT WILL TAKE TO WRITE IT?

Create your book in less than a day with our ***Talk Your Book*** ™ ***creation system***. You simply speak your ideas following an outline that we create for you. Our editorial team puts your ideas on paper. You review, revise, and finally, approve your manuscript. We help you add the finishing touches, and you become a published author in just a few months!

ARE YOU READY TO PUBLISH YOUR MANUSCRIPT?

If you have a manuscript, even *partly* finished, our seasoned team will edit and polish your book with your guidance and input. We use your ideas to create a professional cover design, inviting cover copy, and custom graphics or illustrations for your book's interior. Finally, with our ***Launch Your Book*** ™ ***publishing system*** we'll distribute your book to more than 25,000 bookstores and online retailers. Your life will be forever changed from this point on!

HAVE YOU INVESTED IN A BOOK BUT HAVEN'T THOUGHT ABOUT HOW TO KEEP THE MARKETING MOMENTUM GOING?

Our done-for-you **Book The Business™ marketing system** gives you the marketing tools you need to make your book a success. You simply provide us with your book or other content, and we provide the marketing tools and support. Then, watch your presence grow with ongoing marketing, speaking opportunities, and publicity.

IS IT TIME TO MAKE MORE MONEY FROM YOUR BOOK?

With our **Monetize Your Book™ online learning system**, we help you convert your book or speeches into engaging, self-paced online courses for you to sell on your website. We work with you to develop a course structure, tape your presentation in our professional studio, and monetize your course online. Before you know it, you'll be making money while you sleep.

WITH OUR HELP, IN A FEW SHORT MONTHS, YOU CAN JOIN THE RANKS OF PUBLISHED AUTHORS.

You can add this title to your biography, website, and business card. You can enjoy the benefits a book provides—from new opportunities and increased income, to free publicity and celebrity status—as hundreds of Advantage authors have.

Or, you can maintain the status quo.

The choice is yours. So why not contact us at advantagefamily.com and tell us how we can help you best? Your new opportunities begin with this first step.

"The most remarkable thing about Advantage isn't the physical book, but their remarkable people. When they talk about the 'Advantage Family,' they really mean it. I have never worked with a publisher that invests so much time and effort into creating a positive 'author experience.' I know a winning team when I see one, and the Advantage team is a winner. I can recommend Advantage to you without hesitation."

PAT WILLIAMS
Orlando, Florida

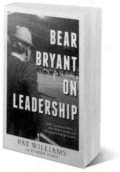

—**Pat Williams**

Co-Founder, Orlando Magic

Author, *Bear Bryant on Leadership* and five other Advantage titles

ADAM D. WITTY

 Adam Witty is the Founder and Chief Executive Officer of Advantage Media Group, a publisher of business, self-improvement, and professional development books and online learning. Adam has worked with hundreds of entrepreneurs, business leaders, and professionals to help them Write, Publish, Market, and Monetize a book to grow their business.

Adam is an in-demand speaker and consultant on marketing and business development techniques for entrepreneurs and authors. Adam is a co-author of *The Book Itch: How to Leave Your Legacy to the World*. Adam has been featured in *The Wall Street Journal, Investors Business Daily, Fortune* magazine, and on ABC and Fox and was named to the 2011 *Inc.* magazine 30 Under 30 list of "America's coolest entrepreneurs." In 2012, Adam was selected by the Chilean government to judge the prestigious Start-up Chile! Entrepreneurship competition.

Adam loves to hear from readers. To connect:

Adam D. Witty

c/o Advantage Media Group

65 Gadsden Street

Charleston, SC 29401

843.701.4943

awitty@advantageww.com

REGISTER YOUR BOOK

AND ACCESS FREE RESOURCES FOR POTENTIAL AUTHORS!

It doesn't matter where you are in the world, Adam can help you share your Stories, Passion, and Knowledge with the world in the form of a published book.

Visit THE21WAYSBOOK.COM/REGISTER to
access these free resources:

 RECEIVE a subscription to the Author Success University™ and Insights with Experts™ monthly teleseminars wherein successful authors and book marketing experts reveal their tips and tricks for marketing and growing a business with a book

 REGISTER for a webinar led by Adam Witty: "How to Quickly Write, Publish, And Profit From A Book That Will Explode Your Business"

 COMPLETE Advantage's Publishing Questionnaire and receive a complimentary Discovery Call with an acquisitions editor to help you determine if your ideas, concepts, or manuscript are worth turning into a book

ACCESS ALL OF THE ABOVE FREE RESOURCES BY REGISTERING YOUR BOOK AT
THE21WAYSBOOK.COM/REGISTER